Twin Flames:

Finding Your Ultimate Lover

JEFF AND SHALEIA

Jeff Ender and Shaleia Clare Divine

(Together permanently and in Harmonious Twin Flame Union
since January 2014)

Master Twin Flame Spiritual Teachers

Jeff and Shaleia Divine
Twin Flames: Finding Your Ultimate Lover
3rd Edition, November 2020

Twin Flames Universe.com books, MP3s,
e-Courses and recorded classes are available.
For details contact Twin Flames Universe at
TwinFlamesUniverse.com

Editor: Yoreen Marcin
Cover Photograph: Shaleia Clare Divine

Twin Flames Universe.com, Inc.
Teaching Twin Flame Union as an Ascension Path to the Divine

To Our Twin Flame Ascension School students who were the first to believe in us and our work. We love you more than you could possibly know. We dedicate this book to you, to our future students, and to our readers. May the consciousness of Harmonious Twin Flame Union transmitted in each page forever remain with you, growing like a Divine Seed of Awareness into ultimate perfection. May you forever recognize with certainty our love for you and our love for your Twin Flame Union.

To God Our Holy Creator, without you, nothing is possible. We love you completely, and we are your happy servants in love, now and forever. Thank you for filling our innocent hearts with your love and teachings, and for showing us the way to helping others into their permanent Harmonious Twin Flame Union. Our love, loyalty, and adoration for you is unwavering, eternal, and complete, as we know for absolute certainty your love for us reflects the same.

Faithfully & Eternally Yours, Always,
Jeff & Shaleia

Contents

Chapter 10 – Colby and Keely's Twin Flame Love Story 161

Twin Flame Decrees   205

Twin Flame Poems   207

Afterword   211

Foreword

Twin Flames: Finding Your Ultimate Lover came as a result of Jeff and I recognizing a profound desire for people to find their Ultimate Lover. More and more every day, people are discovering the truth and reality of Twin Flame Union, while wondering if they have a Twin Flame. In spiritual truth, you do have a Twin Flame, and it is possible and inevitable to re-unite and create a wonderful life-long partnership and sacred union; one that is deliciously satisfying and incredibly meaningful.

There has been a desire climaxing within the collective consciousness of people at this time for a love life not based off of an old paradigm of relating, but one based on real unconditional and Divine Love. Less than a hundred years ago, the idea of marrying for love was considered illogical, and a convenience at best that few ever had. This is the case for the majority of the history of the institution of marriage. Marriage was not a space to fall in love, but rather, a social and cultural contract to fulfill duties society expected. Also, women's roles at that time were only bound to family and marriage (known as the home sphere), and their roles were made by the agreeing authorities in society, because women were perceived as property and treated as such.

Luckily, society today is changing, especially with the Women's Rights Movement legalizing no-fault divorce in 1969, and demanding equal job opportunities. Many women have since taken that opportunity to leave their marriages, and begin creating a life of love they knew they deserved and desired for a long time. Men are free in these new circumstances as well, to truly choose to marry for love, rather than obligation.

In a society that was never taught to marry for love, how do we change the deeply ingrained patterns of not only choosing to marry or partner with someone for love, but creating and maintaining a true unconditional love that transcends the physical into the spiritual? People are desiring more and different things from their relationships than previously in history. Everyone on the planet has a Twin Flame. There is an innate and undeniable desire to be partnered in life with our Ultimate Lover, who is our Twin Flame. We have the desire because of the primal condition of being created with a Twin Flame. That desire never leaves until it's fulfilled.

Deep inside of ourselves we've always felt a perfect soul complement for us, who is not merely a soul mate coming in and out of our eternal existence to share a lesson and an experience with, but a soul who is created from the **exact same blueprint as us**, and who is eternally our spiritual partner, teacher, student, friend and lover. Knowing that everyone on the planet, including yourself, has a Twin Flame, how can you attract spiritual love? By making a different choice than what you've been making previously, which resulted in you experiencing repetitive, unhappy, and unfulfilled relationships and marriages.

Many marriages and relationships are made from a sense of lack within which results in codependency, and is a false, conditional love. This false love was how people "fell in love" when marrying for love finally became socially acceptable and the new norm. This false love is not real because it is not based on Spirit, or soul-to-soul love, but rather, it is dictated by physical, sexual, and personality attraction. All extremely surface level "love" that people decide to marry on and create a family and a life with.

How does this foundation create a stable and lasting relationship? It doesn't. We end up trying to fix the other person, rather than looking within ourselves, taking responsibility for the choices we make, by creating new decisions for ourselves that will give us the desired results we seek. **The choices, decisions, and guidance we act upon is important because it shapes our lives and impacts people around us.**

Luckily, there is an opportunity to change all of this, because each one of us deserves and desires our beloved Twin Flame, and to experience a happy eternal Union. Do not doubt that as you desire this for yourself, your Twin Flame desires this too. In choosing to do the inner work of the *Mirror Exercise* as described in this book, you'll experience the eternal reward of not only living a happy and peaceful life, but clearing old debris hiding in the shadows of your consciousness that is preventing you from your Union, and experiencing a real and meaningful eternal love life with your Twin Flame.

When you and your Twin Flame decide to unite and share a life together in love, it's as if you know in your entire being that this is the way your life should always be, and has been. You feel completely loved, accepted, understood, cherished, and supported in

Who You Are, and in your Divine Life Purpose together. There's a satisfaction and deep longing fulfilled. There are so many avenues of growth, and incredible unending levels of loving and depth to explore and discover together. There is a shared awareness that naturally occurs as you both become more conscious of each other as One. Areas in your life where you thought a romantic partner could never complement you are completely fulfilled in your Union because your Twin Flame is *designed* to complement you there for a specific purpose and reason. Your Twin Flame has the ability to "meet you where you live" spiritually and emotionally like none other. A sense of deep eternal unified purpose exists in a Twin Flame Union. In your Union, you feel at Home because you are One in love with God.

The love life you desire and deserve to have is closer than you think. The manifestation of your desire for your Twin Flame in spiritual union is natural and bound to happen, because God created the desire within you and naturally created you together as One. As you keep your Faith in the process of your manifestation, and experience the rewards and relief of clearing your blocks to your Twin Flame by doing the *Mirror Exercise* in the book, you will open all the doors necessary to invite your Twin Flame Union into your reality with ease and grace, and forever in harmony. Never to experience separation again.

Know your Twin Flame desires to be with you too, and as you continue to heal your barriers to love inside yourself, they too experience that same healing, which helps bring your Union closer together. Furthermore, when you inevitably meet or have met and are working toward Harmonious Twin Flame Union, you will be equipped with the correct tools to not only deepen your love and loving in your Union, but build and maintain an eternal foundation upon which you may experience your Heaven on Earth.

SHALEIA
(pronounced "Shah-lee-ya")

Introduction

"Lovers don't finally meet somewhere.
They're in each other all along."

-RUMI

There is an unseen Power guiding our every thought and action. It is so mighty, that it can bring you anything you desire if you understand how to work with it. Finding your Twin Flame without the use of this Power is an impossible task, but with it, it is inevitable. Only through the use of this Power can one find their Twin Flame and attain Harmonious Twin Flame Union.

Your brain consists of two hemispheres: left and right. This book is written to speak to both hemispheres at once. You may notice the way this book is written may feel uncomfortable to you at times. This is because it is designed to speak to a balanced mind. The discomfort you may experience is actually a re-balancing of your mind. It's a gentle and beneficial side effect of reading the words printed on the following pages. This same discomfort you may experience is also the magnetizing of your mind into harmony with your Twin Flame if you choose to invite them into your life. Naturally passing through this discomfort is a necessary experience which indicates to you that your mind has been properly magnetized and attuned to Higher Vibrational Energies.

You know exactly who your Twin Flame is in your heart, even if you haven't met them yet. Your heart is already programmed to know them, and in spiritual truth, your heart does know your Twin Flame. Practically, no one can tell you who your Twin Flame is. Only you can know, but you can align to those who know the energy because they have mastered it and live permanently in their Harmonious Twin Flame Union. They can help you recognize your Twin Flame, but ultimately, you must go on your inner hero's journey and find out for yourself. These pages were written to help you find them.

Chapter 1

What Are Twin Flames?

She messaged me that night. "You horny?" I blinked at my computer screen. This woman is *ridiculous!* "Always," I replied while brushing her off. What kind of woman messages a man for the first time like that? She doesn't even know me. Of course, we had been Facebook friends for a year. I commented something on a few of her photos, for instance, I thought she was "weirdly sexy." But really, that's all that came of it. And now this. I have so many other women interested in me, and she doesn't look like America's next top model.

But the conversation continued, and before I realized it I didn't even have a chance of shaking off this connection. I ignored her the best I could, but she wanted me to pursue her. I thought to myself, "Yeah, tough luck cookies, I'm busy with nine million other women pursuing me. Why would I make it harder on myself than it needs to be?" But the conversation with her continued, and within 30 minutes of talking to her, I had done something I never had done before in my 26 years of babe-hunting. I asked her to marry me.

This was half a joke at the time, but looking back, I realized there was something different about this kooky chick with a very forward, yet strangely reserved interest in me. It was like she was Queen of the Amazon, only with a slightly weirder appeal. There was something I couldn't refuse about her, something that kept my mind reeling, and my heart coming back for more. But anyway, she was cool, and we were just going to be friends. She lived half the Pacific Ocean away and I lived in Babe Capitol of Hawaii. I didn't need to bother with trying to girlfriend-zone her, but I had fun talking with her.

After our first conversation online nothing much happened for two weeks. I mean, sure, we did have a really good conversation. And yeah, I really did enjoy talking to her. But there were so many things in the way for me not being into her. Two weeks later, she reached out to me again. Today, she would tell me that it was more of a "Hey dude, aren't you going to pursue *this* Queen?" For me, it seemed more like a friendly "Hello." I'm a guy who had long hair, was almost naked all the time, and lived in my own little jungle palace built from bamboo I cut down. I felt like women should be pursuing *me*. But then she offered me a psychic card reading. I was a sucker for psychic card readings, and it was the most accurate reading I had ever received. She was the clearest psychic I had ever talked to. She made me promise not to tell anyone about her gifts. She didn't like being turned into anyone's personal psychic.

This woman had spunk, I'd give her that, and I really enjoyed talking with her. But there was something in her voice, something in the way she carried herself, something in the interests she pursued, and the choices she made, that beat me over the head with "I've gotta get to know her better." We have never stopped talking since that card reading. Not a day goes by that I don't passionately seek to love her more deeply into the very essence of who she is.

Not a day goes by that I don't thank God for bringing her to me. Not a day goes by that I do not want to passionately make love to every inch of her perfectly delicious femininity. That crazy Amazonian Queen… she is my Twin Flame.

What Are Twin Flames?

Twin Flames are manifested from the very same *soul essence,* or more accurately, the same *soul blueprint.* A soul blueprint is the exact same concept as physical DNA. Meaning, our souls are created with individual specific codes, qualities, and traits that make us uniquely us. As above, so below, is a universal law and principle. Just as we have physical DNA that make up our physical genetics and disposition, so too, do we have soul "DNA" that make us who we are spiritually and non-physically. A good example of this is how physical identical twins share the same genetic DNA, and "Twin" Flames share the exact same soul "DNA" or soul blueprint. And just as identical twins are unique as souls even though they share the same physical DNA, Twin Flames are unique among each other even though they share the same soul blueprint. This is because together they are complements to the one soul blueprint rather than carbon copies of it.

Think of your Twin Flame Union as the ancient yin yang symbol: one half is the divine masculine and the other half is the divine feminine, and the little circles inside each half represent the truth that you are not dualistic, but unified as a whole. This is one of the main explanations of your intense attraction and desire for your Twin Flame, because you are created with the same "stuff." And this is also the reason why you possibly cannot ever "merge" with your Twin Flame. You are both already created whole and complete in Divine Perfection as One (like the yin yang symbol), and your journey back to each other is only ever about recognizing that truth. That feeling you do get when you consciously connect to your Twin Flame energy is precisely that, your Twin Flame Union energy (your soul blueprint), and is not a merging of any kind. You can't merge with someone who you are already One with.

Once again, you and your Twin Flame are already complete and whole in Perfection, and your primary block is releasing the belief you are separate in any way from your Twin Flame. Your Twin Flame is created by God at the exact same moment; and they're designed as your soul's highest and most perfect eternal complement.

I'm not a woo-woo kind of guy, but I have always been passionate about finding a woman I could invest my Life Force into; a kind of woman who would keep safe all my secrets and grow with me throughout this life and maybe into the next, if I really believed in that kind of thing. I stumbled upon the jackpot of all jackpots. The perfect woman of an eternal lifetime. She had class, she was funny, she challenged me in a way that stoked my fire, and she was connected to her spirituality, which interested me very much. Shaleia has been with me by my side for every moment of my life since that fateful card reading.

Do I Have a Twin Flame?

Shaleia and I didn't just happen upon each other randomly. There was a **conscious process** each of us followed in order to prepare ourselves and make way for our Twin Flame Union. What you might be wondering is, "How do I know if I have a Twin Flame?" This is really simple to answer. The answer is Yes. A big, fat, huge, resounding "Yes." Yes, of course. You do indeed have a Twin Flame. How can I know while maintaining the integrity of this book, that you have a Twin Flame?

Because you are reading these words.

There is something inside of you that is searching for your Twin Flame, because you innately know you have a Twin Flame. If finding a special partner has absolutely no interest or intrigue to you whatsoever, you wouldn't bother picking up this book, much less reading the first sentence. But you have proven to yourself by making it this far that you do have a Twin Flame, and the Divine created you with a Twin Flame for a very special purpose.

Just as much as you crave, long for, desire, and intimately dream of your perfect lover, so too, does your perfect lover crave, long for, desire, and intimately dream of you. It is just that simple and true.

If you have a desire in your heart for a relationship that transcends the love that we have been taught as a culture, to a love that is created in Heaven, you have a Twin Flame.

Chapter 2

How Do I Find My Twin Flame?

Finding out if you have a Twin Flame is easy. Finding your Twin Flame, that takes a little more effort. But don't worry, this book was written to take you all the way through the whole process to finding your Twin Flame. First, let's go deeper into what a Twin Flame actually is. Getting clear on where we're going is a pretty logical place to start a journey.

I am a Divine Channel, and I am a reasonably logical and grounded individual. I need a LOT of proof to be able to believe that something is real. It has to work in the real world, it has to line up with all my other proven understandings and it has to be supported by grounded, real world results. Well, my channeling has passed all the tests for me. After using it to help heal people of their physical ailments and dis-eases, profoundly resolve the childhood traumas of myself and others, and powerfully impact the lives of those who received my divinely channeled messages, I have carefully been led into a world where Spirit and I have conversations. A world where my Twin Flame comes down the stairs giggling into my office to sit on my lap, and smooch me while I'm writing a book on Twin Flames. A world where Divine Mother-Father God moves through my mind to share His\Her thoughts to accurately describe what Twin Flames are.

What Are Twin Flames? (Channeled)

Twin Flames are the manifestation of the desire to have an eternal companion other than God. Twin Flames were created by Source to have absolute and complete companionship with another soul, because soul mates come and go but your Twin Flame is forever with you sharing Eternal Life, and they mirror God's Divine Love for you the most clearly.

A long time ago, God imagined what Life would be like if Twin Flames were not created. Souls would have such profoundly contrasting experiences. They would find themselves to be so unique and different from one another, that they would be unable to relate on a constantly intimate level. Souls would move in and out of each other's experiences so quickly, that it would cause a deep longing in consciousness. This hypothetical longing sprung from it a way that every soul could have an intimate companion, someone who would grow and change with them eternally, and forever enjoy the river of life, and the Universe together as One.

Twin Flames are unique because they are always bound to each other. The thoughts, actions, and decisions of a Twin Flame intimately and completely impact the other. They are hardly separate, yet they are each unique and complete unto themselves. One cannot exist without the other because they are so perfectly balanced into each other. The perfection and complexity with which this occurs is impossible to explain, or describe, in much the same way that the beauty and vastness of the Universe is impossible to describe.

You can feel your Twin Flame when you anchor your consciousness into your Heart center, and you feel them there in a way that completes you. "Completes" does not mean "makes you happy." "Completes" means "someone who makes you more than you already are in expression, more than you already are in desire, and more than you already are in your Life Force."

You have a Twin Flame, and you know deep in your heart you cannot be the fullest expression of who you really are without your Twin Flame. Many Earth souls have taken it upon themselves to not immediately incarnate with their Twin Flame counterparts, and this is the reason why some of you experience physical age differences in your Union. Your Twin Flame will always incarnate on Earth as you are on Earth. Death can only separate you if you choose separation indefinitely. This can only happen if you absolutely choose to numb and deny your innate desire for your Twin Flame, and have no intention of choosing anything but the illusion of separation from your Good and your One True Love. Death is merely a mirror of your choice in separation from the Divine until you choose to self-actualize.

Life on Earth is meant to awake your soul, to shake up the contents of your Mind, and pour forth an entirely new way of Being, which you can take with you elsewhere on your eternal Universal travels. You are meant to be here for a time, and get things aligned, and then move on and explore other parts of this Infinite Vastness. Here on Earth, you are being warned that having and calling in your Twin Flame before you're ready to do the spiritual work of Harmonious Twin Flame Union is generally not advised.

Jeff will tell you later in this book how challenging it is to have your Twin Flame in your life experience even while working the process. It is life-altering in ways that cannot be described. You will, without a doubt, change in ways you could not fathom before, and in time periods you would never expect. Your growth is automatically set to maximum when you invite your Twin Flame into your life experience, and attain Harmonious Twin Flame Union.

Source invites you to invite this energy of your Perfect Divine Complement into your life with a careful understanding of what you are inviting. What you invite is powerful. What you invite is breathtaking. What you invite can and will reshape everything you know to be as "you" into something even more profound and wonderful: who you are in Divine Truth. But this experience can be challenging, beyond which many souls don't care to bother with on Earth. Take the next step on your Twin Flame journey with an understanding of what you invite. You invite *ALL* OF YOU! If you choose and are prepared for a soul-awakening experience of total bliss, harmony, and Divine Love, preceded by a life-changing experience of breakthroughs and releasing your old way of being, then you are prepared to invite your Twin Flame into your life and embark the ascension path of Harmonious Twin Flame Union.

It Starts with Your Desire

Real desire. That's where it all begins; a sincere desire to manifest into your life experience your most perfect Divine Lover now. You are one who cannot be deterred from being with your Perfect

Divine Complement: your Twin Flame. You are one who cannot dream of being without them. You are one who is willing to take on the trials and tribulations with your Twin Flame by your side. If you are one willing to take the challenge, and reap the reward, then you are one who will most certainly attract, and maintain your Union with your Twin Flame for the rest of eternity.

I desire to share with you YOUR story of finding and keeping your Twin Flame. Your Perfect Partner. Your Ultimate Lover of Lovers. I want to hear about YOU basking in the glory of your permanent Harmonious Twin Flame Union. I am compelled to show you the way, and walk with you from your desire, to the manifestation of your Harmonious Twin Flame Union. If you have made it this far in your journey, you have proven that you are committed to perfecting the spiritual process of attracting your Perfect Partner. With perseverance and strength you can, and you most certainly will meet your Twin Flame and have Harmonious Union. You have proven that you are ready to take the first step in achieving your Ultimate Lover experience. Each chapter of this book is a guidepost for you that will bring you one step closer to understanding and experiencing your Perfect Divine Union with your Ultimate Lover.

Twin Flames First Meeting – Jeff's Story

She was only a few minutes away. After years of fizzled passionate affairs, lost relationships, painful heartbreaks, and seemingly wasted love interest investments, I was finally meeting my Twin Flame for the first time in this lifetime. I pretended to play it cool. But inside, the calm and confident Jeff was shaking. My body was bursting with a mixture of fear, excitement, and utter exhaustion. Maybe it was the 20 hours of traveling which was coming to an end. Maybe it was the airplane food, or the yoga mat, where I had barely managed to grab a nap on the cold morning floor at LAX. Maybe it was the intense four months of online dating I had just completed with my Twin Flame. I was pulsing with emotions and feelings which I was unable to express.

The airport van pulled into the local Comfort Inn motel to drop me off. Looking out the window as we approached the Inn, I saw no one and my heart became anxious. I had been here before, less than a year ago. I had been dropped off alone, and about to meet who I thought was the woman of my dreams. But she wasn't there. And when I made it to her house on my own, she left me alone and stranded on her front porch, refusing to return my phone calls.

Would Shaleia abandon me too? The van left and I found myself once again alone in a parking lot. The familiar feelings of abandonment started to sweep me up as I rolled my luggage toward the other side of the Inn, where I hoped to encounter Shaleia for the first time.

"Jeff!" I heard from behind me. A sweet, clear, feminine voice called out my name as I turned around and saw her in the flesh for the very first time. Wow, she was HOT! I couldn't believe how incredibly attractive she was. My cool and calm disposition was out the window fast as I dropped my bags, cast off my hat, sunglasses, even my sandals, as I sprinted across the parking lot to meet my Ultimate Lover for the very first time in the physical.

Her smile washed across my mind as we melted into each other's arms. We were spinning and twirling, sweetly and gently, yet passionately and full of emotion. This is what coming Home for the first time feels like. My head spun, it felt like I had finally been released into an oxygen-rich environment. All my fears and trepidation faded as I held her close to my chest. Her arms embraced my body and soul, in what was the most epic meeting of my existence.

She would later tell me that she also felt a sense of "coming home," as many Twin Flames describe in their Unions. I always feel and know I'm at home with Shaleia by my side.

The Story Is Real

I love the experience of meeting someone new. Bringing a new person into my life, and exploring the excitement and richness with them. That excitement and richness usually fades away though, and I need to get a new person to experience this sensation with again. With your Twin Flame you may experience this meeting as a peak experience like I did, but why bother? Won't you just get bored of this person like all the rest? Won't this person treat you like all the rest have? Won't this person discard you like all the rest? Then what are you left with? While all of the above are legitimate concerns, I can show you why they are irrelevant for your Harmonious Twin Flame Union. It is called a Union, rather than a relationship, because a Union is a more accurate term to describe what is actually occurring. In a typical soul mate relationship, two people relate to one another from the two different shores of their souls. The relationship will end at some point in "time," and they perhaps move on to another relationship in another lifetime or in this one; or perhaps, they finally settle on attracting their permanent Harmonious Twin Flame Union.

Romantic soul mate relationships are inevitably doomed because these souls are not perfectly designed to be with you. This is a good thing because it means someone is: your Twin Flame who is your natural Divine Counterpart. Do not be sad if and when you release your soul mate relationship for your Twin Flame, because in doing so you free yourself to be with your One True Love, and you are releasing your soul mate to be with theirs. This is what true love and compassion in action looks like, and you role-model to the younger generations the importance of choosing your Twin Flame Union only, rather than settling for less than you deserve.

A Harmonious Union is a coming together of a soul's counterpart in a permanent and unbreakable eternal commitment/vow. You are not complete without your Twin Flame, but you absolutely are always whole. You do not need to have your Twin Flame in your life to be whole, but you do need them to feel totally complete and to experience all of you being expressed through your one Union. This sense of incompleteness can become unbearable, and this may be one reason why you are reading this book; to restore your own sense and truth of completeness.

Twin Flames and the Mirroring Effect Explained

There is no need for another lover ever when you have finally met your Twin Flame. This person will fill all the desires you have for an intimate partner, even if your list of desires is extensive. The energy of your desires and "needs" are highly and fully concentrated in your Twin Flame Union. This person may even do all the same challenging things as many of your previous lovers, because they are helping you to release old patterns and traumas existing within your Mind thus preventing you from your Harmonious Twin Flame Union. They do this out of love and compassion for you, and for your experience and desire for wholeness. They do not do this because they are cruel, abusive, hateful, or desire to destroy the Union. They do this to heal you and to heal themselves. Your experience with your Twin Flame will be unique and completely your own understanding. Twin Flames always experience exactly what they need together.

Each story is different, but one thing that is always the same in Twin Flame Union is that they will bring up each other's "stuff." What do I mean by "stuff?" It's the childhood traumas, upsets, and pains; and it's the misaligned thoughts, patterns and limiting beliefs we find ourselves stuck in. Essentially, it's the out-of-alignment with love and our Divine Self decisions that we've been making over and over again, sometimes repeating lifetime after lifetime in a repetitious karmic cycle.

When this "stuff" comes up to the surface, it's often very uncomfortable because you are strongly attached on some level to your ego story, but you're encouraged by your Twin Flame to look at it and clear it. Why do they seem to upset you? Because they love you, and because they *are* you! They desire to see you grow and become the best version of you – your Divine Self – that you can be. They are also intrinsically motivated to do so, because they are so intimately interwoven with you, and they too, desire to be the best version of themselves. This is basically what we call the *Twin Flame Mirroring Effect.*

Mirroring occurs directly throughout your Twin Flame Union because you and your Twin Flame share the same One Consciousness. They must mirror any and all core choices and beliefs you have, and vice versa, until a new core choice is made. When that choice is aligned to Divine Love you will experience your reality and Twin Flame mirroring that loving choice. Each loving choice you make in your reality is the stepping stone to your permanent Harmonious Twin Flame Union. This *Mirroring Effect* also explains why it's impossible for one Twin to be so-called "awakened" and the other is not. Your Twin Flame is equally awakened as you are because you are One. They are not your carbon copy. This means they will be awakened or aware in certain areas where you are not and vice versa, but it doesn't mean that they are not on the same level as you spiritually. They most definitely are, and to believe differently is to believe that you can be separate from your Twin Flame. Your Twin Flame is as much your highest spiritual teacher as they are your highest spiritual student. And any good student is astute in learning what the teacher is sharing so that they can master the lessons.

The *Twin Flame Mirroring Effect* exists solely as a reflection of your personal relationship with God, who is your Divine Creator in heaven. That's one of the main functions of your Twin Flame Union: to reflect to you your relationship, choices and consciousness regarding your Divine Creator. This is truly the one piece that many struggle with on their Twin Flame journey. People want to point the finger at their Twin Flame and blame them for the reason they're upset and why they're not together, but by spiritual law, your Twin Flame is reflecting your upsets with God and with yourself. Resolve these upsets, and you resolve your separation from your Twin Flame. We go into great detail how to do this later on in the book.

I invite you not to feel disheartened at the reality of the upsets your Twin Flame will bring up for you. As you master the spiritual tools and consciousness we share with you in this book, and on our online classes and e-Courses at TwinFlamesUniverse.com, the easier it is to enjoy your Twin Flame and attain your permanent Harmonious Union. To attain the "permanent" aspect of your Harmonious Twin Flame Union, you must commit to healing your upsets as they arise; and know that it does get easier and easier, and it does feel better working on yourself spiritually with your Twin Flame by your side in the physical. In fact it's even more rewarding to accomplish your spiritual work while in Harmonious Union together, because you share your process, feelings, love, and joy as they arise.

Is there an end to experiencing upsets in your Twin Flame Union? Absolutely! As you progress further and further into your Harmonious Twin Flame Union, you will eventually arrive together to a state we call "Perfect Union," also known as, ascension. We speak more of this important ultimate end goal in another chapter.

If you're genuinely looking for the most intimate experience you can have with another human being possible, look no further, your Twin Flame is exactly that. This is not an illusion, this isn't hype, and it's not "woo-woo." This is the wonderful and the Divine, and it's life-transformation with challenges designed to grow you and deepen your experience of being with your Twin Flame. If you're willing to take the challenging, along with the ecstatic, then you're not only on the right track, but you have the correct attitude to finding your Twin Flame and living your perfect Heaven on Earth in Harmonious Union together.

Your Twin Flame *will* bring up all of your "stuff" and sometimes at what feels like an alarming pace, but you are 100 percent in control of how quickly, or slowly, you enter your Harmonious Twin Flame Union. If you're not equipped with some very powerful tools to help you move through the **upset phase** of your Union, then you're going to have a tough time. Shaleia and I went through the very hard stuff, and we were able to pave a relieving path that is clear and easy for you. We did this consciously because we knew the gravity of the situation we had chosen to create for ourselves. We forged a way through the darkest hours of the Twin Flame experience, and emerged from Union to Harmonious Twin Flame Union; and we are here to hand you the tools to your liberation as well.

But before we work on that together, let's begin with this very simple yet deep question: How will you know when you've met your Twin Flame?

Chapter 3

How Will I Know when I've Met My Twin Flame?

There is a way to determine who your Twin Flame is, but patience is required as you go through the spiritual revealing process. We discuss how doing a Love List (in a later chapter) helps validate who your Twin Flame is, and of course a deep certainty based on actual familiarity with this person, asking God for very clear and understandable signs, visions through meditating, and learning how to correctly use the pendulum. We caution against using psychic services to identify your Twin Flame, only because the clear majority of psychics currently out there are not correctly attuned to Twin Flame energy, or correctly attuning 100 percent to the Divine (even if they say so or have the best of intentions) that would help them validate for you your Twin Flame. Having your Twin Flame revealed to you is incredibly sacred, and the ability for someone outside of you to actually validate your true Twin Flame, is in spiritual truth, a Divine Miracle being performed. I do not say this lightly, nor am I simply being a spiritual connoisseur, or making this up for the sake of it; but what I know for sure is to be able to successfully see and recognize true Twin Flames is a miracle performed by and through the Divine only. The reason why only certain individuals are bestowed with the ability to perform this miracle is because you have to be absolutely aligned to perfect

Divine Love with God, and undeniably recognize the energy pattern of the exact same resonating soul blueprint of the individuals.

At the time of this writing, it is still fairly easy for frauds to pretend to be Twin Flames, because so few are able to see truly and clearly actual Union. That is why it is so important to follow us and our work, and only choose to listen to teachers, healers, and coaches who remain within our spiritual community and lineage.

It is difficult at first to identify Twin Flames because it requires *being able to see clearly with your heart.* At first, only a blurry blinding light would indicate to you that something might be there. With more experience and growth you will begin to gain assurance and clarity, that yes, this is definitely a Twin Flame set. As your spiritual sight grows more clear and attuned to the specific energy wave pattern of Twin Flames, you may be able to pick out true Twin Flames here and there with some accuracy. Eventually, you'll usually be able to tell fairly well. But after a certain point of becoming clearer in your heart's vision, you will be able to see Twin Flames just as clearly as if someone were to turn on a light in a dark room and ask you whether it was light or dark in the room.

Ultimately, regardless of whether you are initially correct in determining a specific individual as your true Twin Flame or not, you must go through the revealing process and *experience* your Twin Flame Union as your truth. This might be why you could get resistance from your Twin if you tell them you are Twin Flames without them coming to the conclusion of the connection themselves. It's one thing to say you're Twins, and a whole other thing to get in the driver's seat and test out the truth and eternal indestructibility of your Union. Remember, Twin Flame Union is a Divine Love, so the one common and ongoing theme you will experience with and from your Twin Flame experience is this:

"Do you love me unconditionally? Even if I choose something in my experience that triggers you? Will you love me no matter what? Will you always choose to love me, or do you just want something from me?"

Truth is, you're asking your Twin Flame the exact same questions in your vibration, and you must respond with the unconditional love you are seeking from them to yourself and to your Twin. They will respond and mirror to you your core choice of unconditional love for them and yourself, whether it's an inner feeling or an external change or sign. When you choose love and closeness, so does your Twin Flame, but if you truly in your heart choose love and closeness with each upset you are healing, but your partner simultaneously chooses fear and separation, then it's likely a sign of a *false Twin Flame*.

One of the reasons why you could mistake a false Twin Flame for your actual Twin Flame, is because a false Twin always appears on the outside, and sometimes on the personality-level, like they are your true Twin Flame. This is the unique signature they possess that coins them as a false Twin Flame and easily sways you into believing they are your true Twin. This is why the revealing process is so important. I call it the revealing process because you have to go through the spiritual journey of meeting your Twin Flame both on the inner and outer world. You cannot avoid it with a flick of a magic wand that says "here's your true Twin Flame!"

God works in mysterious ways, and as much as we may think we are with our Twin Flame, they might be a false Twin Flame. Don't be alarmed, because the false Twin Flame has a very special and specific purpose as a gateway experience to your true Twin Flame. One of the other purposes of your false Twin Flame is to reveal to you all your major blocks and upsets to your true Twin Flame. You would be wise to meditate and journal on what these lessons are, and then heal what arises from these lessons. We share with you how to do that with the *Mirror Exercise* explained later. Both Shaleia and I had false Twin Flame experiences, which led directly to our true Twin Flame. We both believed without a shadow of a doubt that the person at hand was our true Twin Flame, and it had to be in order for the both of us to go through the experience that would eventually lead us into each other's lives.

Jeff's False Twin Flame Story

Sophia just left Hawaii, and honestly I was glad to be rid of her. She spent two months living, working, and loving with me in my jungle cabin. She helped me build my bed and breakfast, helped me design the idea for bringing in a new consciousness to the property I lived on, and helped update the cabin with new carpet while adding a feminine touch. She even happily engaged in some relationship and spiritual work with me.

I really loved having a woman like that around. I thought I wanted to have kids with her, and maybe marry her one day. I thought I wanted her back again, but deep down I knew I didn't like having her around at all. There was something off about her... and yet I couldn't stop my heart from longing for her.

I've done a reasonable amount of meditation to know when my feelings are transcendental, and when they are coming from hormonal chemical reactions in my brain. There was something seriously wrong in my heart for days and weeks following her exodus from my life. Now, she was half an ocean away and tucked back in the redwood forests of Northern California. A very comfortable distance for someone you dislike, but a very painful stretch for your True Love. I didn't know at the time that the pain in my chest, that strong "off" feeling I was having, was the sacred calling of my Twin Flame Lover.

My heart was broken from the absence of Sophia, even though the rest of me felt very good about it. I had a new found energy and zest for life. I even quadrupled the size of my jungle cabin in the weeks following her departure. But, when I tuned into my heart, I knew it was calling Sophia's name. I can do little to control my heart when it leads me somewhere. It has been my main source of direction for many years now, and when it calls I know enough to listen.

I called Sophia shortly after and expressed my passionate and undying love for her. I described how the distance and separation made me clear about my love for her, and no matter what it took, we had to be back together again. Her response back was lackluster and slightly disheartening to me, but it didn't stop me either. I knew I had to win her heart back at any cost. I thought I had broken her heart and hurt her by breaking up with her when I asked her to leave my place.

It wasn't long before she warmed up to me again and let me call her my girlfriend. In this warm period, I purchased a plane ticket to go see her with money I barely had. I knew I had to do it though, because my heart called and it was leading me to my destiny. But things got rocky shortly thereafter, and she stopped talking to me two weeks before I flew out. It seemed she was doing everything she could to hurt me and prevent me from loving her. My heart was seriously wounded, but it still called her name. I believed being in my presence would strongly clear her mind. I had never before been so wildly passionate about loving someone. Never before was my heart so clear and keen, even despite massive attack and wounding from its beloved.

Sophia took up a new dance partner to keep her mind off me. I knew I could sweep her off her feet from any man though, even if he was passionate about Brazilian dance, and spoke Sophia's native language. By the time I arrived, her sentiment had me extremely disheartened. I wasn't going to give up without knowing precisely the way she felt and why she felt that way. All along my heart was telling me that she loved me; except I would soon find out that she didn't.

Her new boyfriend, the dance partner, was all she could talk about during my visit and she wouldn't have anything to do with me. I even met the guy (to my heart's tremendous pain and trauma). Eventually, it became very clear; and I knew I had to let Sophia go.

I experienced peace on the train ride back down to LA, as I knew my heart had not failed me or led me astray. Something tremendously positive must come as a result of all this. I was aware that all of my heartbreak and pain was leading me toward something wonderful and delicious. Oh, how right that quiet voice was, and oh, how difficult it was to listen to this inner voice after all my pain with Sophia.

I arrived home to my jungle cabin in Hawaii and I moved on with my life. I even started seeing a different woman. She helped, but of course it didn't last. Before I knew it though, I was back to my full Self. I had scarcely forgotten Sophia the day Shaleia instant messaged me for the first time.

Shaleia's False Twin Flame Story

Since 2010 I had been deliberately seeking and spiritually preparing myself for my Twin Flame and our Harmonious Union. Two years later I had moved across the country to Sedona, Arizona. I was confident I was at the epicenter of spiritual community, especially with all the spiritual vortex energies in and around Sedona. I had no doubt I would meet the man of my dreams here. Little did I know there was a half-truth to that thought. It just didn't happen in the way I expected it to.

Before I met my false Twin, Jake, I told my spirit guides I desired to be in my Twin Flame Union as soon as possible. I was 28 years old, and I didn't want to wait any longer to be with him than I had to. My spirit guides (who were also Twin Flames) told me it was possible, but

I would need to make a choice: either I can slow-track to my Union or fast-track it. Slow would've been more easy and gentle in a sense, although longer to attain my Union, but I was ready to end separation with my Twin Flame as soon as possible. I've already been 28 years without him, so let's get the show on the road! That was my attitude. I wanted it to be quick, so I chose the fast-track route. But what did taking the shortcut actually mean? I didn't ask because I didn't care due to my strong desire for my Harmonious Twin Flame Union now.

This is partly why I attracted my false Twin Flame, it's a shortcut to clear old energy blocks and patterns I had in relationships, and enable me to vibrate to a place where I could attract my true Twin Flame. When I met Jake I believed strongly he was my Twin Flame because of how he presented himself to me, and so it was true for me. I believed all the signs were there, even justifying so-called synchronicity when I missed – actually I denied – all the real signs that he **wasn't** my true Twin Flame.

He was the stereotypical attractive hippie guy who seemed to be on the leading edge of New Age thought (or so I projected). He claimed to be an amazing triple Aquarian sign who ate only super-foods and was into wearing energy medicine necklaces. He also assisted in putting together conscious festivals across the West coast circuit. Jake presented himself to be a highly evolved conscious man, who could keep up with my spiritual growth and path because he was diligently on his.

Oh how I felt deceived when the real truth finally came out! I saw red flag after red flag, and I <u>still</u> purposely ignored them, and focused solely on what I desired to see (this is called self-deception and hence why I experienced being deceived and manipulated). I did not feel empowered or supported in our relationship. All Jake did was take from me and my resources, blame everyone around him, expect me to bend to his will (control me), and systematically take advantage of those around him and play victim when called out.

Within two weeks of meeting Jake at the Sedona Yoga Festival we had moved in together. I was drained around him all the time because he was vamping my energy clean with his neediness and co-dependent behaviors. Whenever we would get into upsets, there was never **any** mutual resolve, no matter how hard I tried to have positive communication and healing with him. He made important decisions for us without consulting or verifying with me, and he had no spiritual ambition or desire to grow individually or as a couple together. He would invite people I didn't know or meet before to stay over at our one bedroom apartment without asking me, and he was not interested in developing our relationship together beyond what it was when we initially met. The only relationship I saw him have was the one he had with his computer. It reminded me greatly of my biological father who used his work, computer, and cell phone as a scapegoat to systematically numb out to his relationships, feelings, and any meaningful connection with Life.

Another major red flag was how open he was with his friends and acquaintances about our relationship and my private business. I realized I was never loved or cherished in his arms, and I only ever had an absent-minded, ungrounded, numbed out, and unconscious partner who stopped dating me the moment he moved in because he got what he wanted. He became very cold and distant quickly. I felt like I was sleeping next to a stranger, because I realized we actually were strangers and we had nothing in common at the core. I allowed *myself to fall for a guy who I thought "looked" and "sounded" like my Twin Flame, but in truth he was very spiritually, emotionally, and financially abusive toward me. When these upsets arose from his maltreatment, I would heal it and choose love, but Jake would only choose separation from me more deeply. I always revealed myself as someone who chooses love and healing, but he consistently revealed to me his choosing of ego and psychosis.*

*I desired a conscious hippie man, but the problem was I **projected** the qualities I desired in a man and tried to fashion him to be who I wanted him to be. Projection occurs when you come from a place of lack within yourself, and create a situation where you attempt to have what you feel lacking fulfilled in something or someone outside of yourself, rather than going to Love (God) and getting it from there. Happiness and joy never come later when you have something, it's a choice and a realization you can only have now inside of yourself.*

We lived together for a month before we split. It was the perfect recipe for heartbreak and breakdowns. But a perfect lesson on thoughts and beliefs I was having out of alignment with my Divine Self and my Harmonious Twin Flame Union; releasing what I thought my ideal partner should look and be like, and learning to only support the Divine in my relationships, rather than the ego. Shortly after we broke up I was in really rough shape. My job at the local Thai restaurant was failing because I was getting less and less hours, and I knew it was a sign I was going to get sacked soon. On top of those previously stressful situations, my new landlord gave me a month's notice to leave because they were selling the house. It was coming up Christmas time and I had no other housing options available in my price range. I felt like I had been on a roller coaster ride from hell dealing with the tumultuous breakup and subsequent aftermath. I decided to utilize this experience and all the changes happening to me to further my spiritual growth and development. I didn't desire to ever attract a false Twin Flame again, or put myself in such a vulnerable position. One false Twin Flame experience is truly all you ever need to receive and understand the lessons they are teaching you to achieve your Harmonious Twin Flame Union. Choose to be kind to yourself and do not go through multiple false Twin Flame relationships. You can do this by choosing to be diligent in what they're mirroring to you and healing that.

In order for me to start to pick up the pieces of my life and move forward again, I practiced the Mirror Exercise my spiritual teacher had taught me, I truly felt all my feelings as they would arise, and I did multiple oracle and tarot card readings for myself to see what the lessons were in that false Union. Most of my lessons had to do with projecting my unfulfilled needs and desires onto another at any personal cost. I knew what God was telling me through the oracle cards was true because I was tired of "being alone," and a part of me was scared that I would be doomed to walk this Earth alone forever. Upon reconnecting with my Divine Relationship with God, I healed the part of me that felt alone and doomed to be uncoupled the rest of my life. These were just a few of the thoughts that were directly creating separation from my true Twin Flame, and hence, why I wasn't attracting him into my physical reality experience. All these lessons my false Twin Flame brought me were beginning to reveal themselves as great gifts of wisdom, awareness, love, and healing. I began to lose my anger and resentment, and instead, developed appreciation and gratitude for what this soul brought me. If it wasn't for Jake, or my choice to fast-

track into my Harmonious Twin Flame Union, I wouldn't be writing this book and helping so many others meet their true Twin Flame and attain their own Harmonious Union today.

Due to the extreme contrast I experienced with Jake, I was incredibly clear about what I desired in my next relationship. I created an extensive two to three page "Love List," that acted as my set of standards when I would be ready to open myself up to dating again, and as a "vision board" of my perfect romantic relationship, and lastly in assisting me in identifying my Twin Flame, because I already know him in my heart. Here are a few examples of what I wrote in my **Love List**:

1. My partner has a thriving and sustainable monthly income that is capable of supporting a family.

2. He is supportive of me physically, emotionally, mentally, spiritually, and supports me being a stay-at-home mother for the formative years of our child's development.

3. He knows his dreams and desires, and actively manifests them into being. He has strength of character, perseverance, and a clear direction in life.

4. He actively puts effort into the daily maintenance of our relationship.

5. He is psychologically and spiritually balanced and well.

6. He has integrity, and he honors his word.

7. There is a natural giving and receiving balance in the relationship.

8. *We are positive role models for other couples and our family.*

9. *He takes 100 percent ownership for his choices – no blaming.*

10. *He is solution-oriented. Whenever we experience challenges in the relationship it doesn't destroy it, but rather, we use challenges as a tool to deepen our relationship.*

11. *He respects my personal space and freedom.*

Upon meditating on my Love List, I realized I am, and also must become, these qualities I desired in my beloved. Recognizing who I am at my core and what I deeply value, will naturally assist me in revealing who my Twin Flame is at their core. You will recognize your Twin Flame by their inner qualities only, and not their outer qualities and appearances (hint, hint*). It took me a full three months after my experience and recovery from my false Twin Flame, before I finally met my real Twin Flame. I knew in my Heart I was truly ready. I had learned my primary lessons from my false Twin Flame, and most importantly, I had forgiven him and myself for all the ego, unloving thoughts, and actions in the relationship. My spiritual teacher would remind me, **"You have to love him before you can leave him."** *This act of awareness and healing is absolutely essential in going deeper in intimacy with your true Twin Flame.*

A couple of months into dating Jeff, I read off my Love List to him over the phone. Everything I read to him he was like, "Yep, yep, yep… that's me!" There were obviously a few things he had not fully become yet (like being a father and achieving great financial independence), but that's because it's a work in progress… something he's in the process of grow-

ing into like I was. I was both floored and very comforted by how he embodied my Love List perfectly. Looking back on it now I'm not very surprised because I've always known in my heart who my Twin Flame was. We are One; and when I went to the place in my heart where we are One it was easy to identify our core values and principles. These core values and principles actually reflect the design of our soul blueprint.

How to Differentiate a False from a True Twin Flame (Channeled)

As a Divine Channel, I am able to ask God to provide some signs to show if you have met your true Twin Flame. This can clarify whether you are with your true Twin Flame or your false Twin. It might be part of your path to experience a false Twin Flame, like Shaleia and I did, in order to clear the obstacles in your way to being with your true Twin Flame although it's not a mandatory experience. Remember, your false Twin Flame can be the gateway to your true Twin Flame when you utilize the lessons, and choose to heal the core blocks your false Twin Flame is presenting for your real Twin Flame Union to occur.

God's Nine Signs You Are with Your True Twin Flame (Channeled):

1. Your Twin Flame will feel familiar to you. Nobody in this world feels as familiar and as comfortable to you as your Twin Flame. Not even your parents equal the familiarity

and kinship you will feel with your Twin Flame. It may feel as though you have been friends for lifetimes, and this is absolutely true. Your closest human friend is your Twin Flame.

2. Your Twin Flame will share the same vision for their life as you do. If you are unclear about everything, so too will your Twin Flame be unclear. They will want all the same things for themselves as you do. They will share a clear vision with you for your lives together if you do the work to create a clear vision. Their personal vision also complements and enhances your own.

3. Your Twin Flame will desire the same things as you from life. They will want to live similar experiences and gain similar understandings. They will not desire everything exactly as you do because they are not a carbon copy of you.

4. Your lifestyle choices will align easily with your Twin Flame if you take the time to get clear on your choices together and individually.

5. Your Twin Flame will value the same things as you when you both get clear on your values. *A good way to uncover a false Twin Flame is to get clear on your values with your partner.* No true Twin Flame will avoid doing the work with you if you are sincere about doing your spiritual work, and getting clear on your values.

6. Your Twin Flame will adore you at the core above all others. A false Twin can have many more love interests, but your true Twin Flame will not genuinely ever love another human as much as they love you. You know you have left

your Twin Flame long ago if you still sincerely love that person with your innermost heart, even if you find it intolerable to be around them.

7. Your true Twin Flame will always love you. You will know this when you tune into your heart center. Your Twin Flame will never abandon you in love, and will never truly withdraw their love. They cannot, because they ARE you.

8. Your true Twin Flame will always genuinely enjoy your company. True Twin Flames feel comfortable and relaxed in each other's honest and authentic presence.

9. When you meditate deeply within your heart you can see if the person in question is an exact vibratory match to your soul's blueprint.

Nine Signs You Are with a False Twin Flame (Channeled)

1. A false Twin Flame will regularly abandon you. They will find ways to split up with you and get away from you either emotionally, spiritually, or physically. They will not be interested in spending long stretches of time with you, because they are not designed to be around you for long sustained periods.

2. A false Twin Flame will try to lie to you about who they really are. They will not want you to know they are false because they get so much love energy from you without having to reciprocate anything real. A false Twin Flame

will likely try to take as much of your love as possible without wanting to give love back.

3. A false Twin Flame will not share your vision for the future.

4. A false Twin Flame will not share *all* your deepest core values with you, nor will they feel inclined to do spiritual work with you to discover your values together.

5. A false Twin Flame will likely try to hide their true selves from you. They will not want to honestly share the deepest parts of themselves with you even if cornered or persuaded to do so.

6. A false Twin Flame will not help you create the vision for your life, nor will they feel inclined to be part of your life's vision.

7. A false Twin Flame will always prevent you from going deeper with them, no matter what you do.

8. A false Twin Flame will not be interested in bringing your painful inner misalignments to the surface. They will be more interested in enjoying your presence now as you are, and not interested in investing in you and helping you become aligned with your Divine Self by bringing your core "stuff" to the surface for healing.

9. On the surface your false Twin Flame appears as your true Twin Flame, but as you go deeper, they reveal to you they are not who you are looking for. As you choose love at core in the upset places inside of yourself your false Twin Flame is mirroring, they'll choose separation over unity, versus your Twin Flame who would mirror your core choice in love and be unified with you.

Conclusion

Whether you have found your false Twin Flame, or your true Twin Flame, you are on the right track to your Eternal Divine Union. The false Twin Flame is an aide to help you prepare for your true Twin Flame Union. Do not fret if you find that your true Twin Flame is married with children to another person. You and your Twin Flame will always have a perfect and harmonious connection deep in your hearts that can never be tarnished. That person may again find a way into your life if you continue to choose to follow the deepest desire for love in your heart. God shapes our lives in mysterious and wonderful ways. If you have in your heart a deep desire for your true Twin Flame Union, then you will soon find that your Twin Flame was waiting there for you all along too, and the steps forward to your Harmonious Twin Flame Union are always revealed in Perfect Divine Order.

Chapter 4

Meeting Your Twin Flame

Shaleia's Twin Flame Meeting Story

I'll never forget how Jeff and I first met. It was truly magical. The room I was renting was clean, organized, and ready to receive him. I wore my favorite red shirt, my makeup looked good, and I had a meal cooked and waiting for him in the crock pot. My roommate said I could borrow her car to pick him up. I was very relieved!

His scheduled drop-off was 5:30pm at the Comfort Inn. I was already waiting there by the allotted time. I was incredibly nervous and excited to meet the man I had been having an epic online relationship with for the past four months. I was chugging coconut water like crazy to help calm my nerves, and I kept checking the car mirror to see if my makeup was okay. Ten long minutes passed before I saw the airport shuttle making its way into the parking lot from my back window. My heart was pounding even harder now in my chest.

The driver got out of her seat to open the back hatch and get Jeff's luggage from the van. I couldn't see Jeff yet from my window, but I knew it was time to get out of the car and introduce myself to him. I walked around the back of the van as the driver was shutting the hatch. I saw

Jeff's back toward me about 20 feet away. He was pulling his luggage behind him, while searching for me at the corner of the motel building. The airport shuttle began pulling out of its parking spot, when I calmly yelled his name, "Jeff!" He immediately shot a glance toward me, and in a split second, with a giant smile on his face, he ran to me while dropping his luggage on the ground, throwing off his hat and sunglasses, and kicking off his shoes. I had never experienced someone so joyful and happy to see me in all my life. I opened up my arms wide to receive him as I kept walking in his direction.

In the blink of an eye, we were holding each other in complete love, unity, and bliss. It was the most Divine and enriching hug I had ever experienced. We remained holding each other for at least a minute long, but it felt longer. In his arms was this feeling of timelessness and everlasting unconditional love. This must be how God is.

Something about his touch reached deeply into my bones, acknowledging to me that he is the One I had been desiring to be with my entire life. My heart was still beating incredibly hard and fast against his chest. I felt this natural energetic exchange occurring between us. There was this HUGE energy of pure love circulating between us in a way I had never experienced with anyone before. Being in his embrace did feel like "home." I thought I had that experience before with another, but not after this experience. It has trumped any old feeling and notion of "home" I may have had with another.

I told Jeff I desired to look him in the eyes. We ended our embrace as our eyes locked, both of us looking lovingly at each other. He was already quite handsome online, but in person he was even more attractive. I felt humbled that I manifested such a deeply loving, spiritual, and physically gorgeous man. Of all the dreams I had for myself, being physically united with my Twin Flame was primary. Tears began quelling in his eyes. I was so touched, that tears were rolling down my cheeks too. I enjoyed seeing Jeff for the first time, and in his eyes too, rather than through a computer screen. The feeling of relief was mutual.

Jeff asked if we could sit on the bench next to the motel entrance and relax for a few minutes. We collected his baggage and sat down while beginning to process the magnum of our meeting. After some time, we decided it would be best for us to continue our uniting at my house. We got back from the motel and I gave him a tour of the house. At the end of the tour we went to my back porch with hot herbal tea in our hands. Somehow I accidentally destroyed our crock-pot dinner, but it didn't matter; we chatted and held hands until the moon and stars were shining brightly in the desert sky, and UFOs were buzzing about the vortexes. Meeting my Twin Flame felt different than anyone else I've ever connected with in my life. It was deeply, deeply powerful and authentic. The best meeting I could have ever hoped or imagined for.

I had my suspicions for months prior that Jeff was my true Twin Flame, especially after reading my Love List to him, and by how I felt when we would talk to each other. The inner and physical feelings I had when we met in the parking lot for the first time had me highly conclusive that Jeff was my true Twin Flame, but I needed further confirmation to safely determine without a doubt that Jeff's my Twin Flame. The very next day I laid down to meditate and connect with my Divine Creator. Almost as soon as I closed my eyes, my third eye burst wide open with a very obvious Twin Flame sign that showed half my face and half of Jeff's face as One Face. It wasn't a "merging" (as that doesn't exist), but a clear and visible sign that I would understand that Jeff was indeed my true Twin Flame. I even heard God's voice whisper in my ear chakras that Jeff is my true Twin Flame, and He said to me that the search is finally over. I sat straight up and looked upon the face of my beloved, and any remaining doubt that I held was completely washed away and replaced with absolute certainty. I had been consciously developing my third eye chakra for over 10 years, so I very much trust the visions from God I receive. I also trusted my spiritual teacher's channeling ability and her relationship with God to further confirm for both of us that we are real Twin Flames.

The Decision before the Meeting

Before you meet your Twin Flame, you need to make a choice. If you truly desire to be with your Ultimate Lover, you're going to need to decide whether you actually want to be with them or not. So, the first step is to choose with your heart to be with your Twin Flame and to have your Harmonious Twin Flame Union.

Those of you who are ready to move forward and be with your Twin Flame may go ahead and do this exercise now. Those of you who are yet unsure, it is safe for you to skip the exercise and come back to it later. It will always be here for you when you are ready.

Attracting Your Twin Flame Meditation Exercise

Take a moment to center and create a space inside yourself. Take a deep breath and relax. It is just as easy to do this exercise with your eyes open or closed. You are welcome to pause and take breaks when visualizing, for as long as it feels good to you.

Slowly take three long inhales and exhales while focusing on your heart center.

When you feel ready with only your imagination to guide you, you will find yourself in a beautiful, peaceful, quiet, and safe space.

You notice something stir nearby. Take a look and see what it is.

It is your Twin Flame. Do you notice their openness toward you?

In order to choose to bring them into your life, all you need to do is invite them to come, and sit next to you. Your subconscious mind knows what it means when you invite your Twin Flame to come sit next to you in this safe place. You have invited your Twin Flame into your life now. If there is anything you desire to say to your Twin Flame, communicate it to them and listen if they have anything to communicate back to you. Continue to spend as much time with your Twin Flame as you desire.

Sit in this energy with your beloved Twin Flame until you feel complete with this exercise.

There is nothing more to do. The exercise is complete, and you have communicated to your subconscious mind and ALL of who you are, the decision you have made to bring your Twin Flame into your life. This is the most important thing you can do to attract your Twin Flame: choose to have them in your life.

Two of the most powerful qualities we have is choice and free will. There is nothing which can take our choice and free will away from us. The innermost tenets of our Being is choice and free will. You have the freedom to choose and your choices have tremendous power, of which, you may not yet even be aware of yet. Choosing to invite your Twin Flame in the exercise above, is choosing to have your Twin Flame in your life permanently. In order to have truly chosen your Twin Flame, you needed first to desire them. Feel free to repeat this exercise any time you feel you have *chosen different-ly*. You can do this exercise as many times as you like, and it's a wonderful way to connect with them while you're in the process of coming together into Harmonious Twin Flame Union.

Attracting Your Twin Flame

You already have the desire for your Twin Flame and you have proven it by investing in materials to assist you toward your Union. Now, whether you've done the exercise or not, we're going to continue to attract your Twin Flame by working through whatever arises within you. You may have already experienced a subtle shift in your reality and energy since learning about this book, and even since picking it up and reading through the pages. You might be feeling different, or not, but one thing's for certain: If you have completed the exercise in choosing your Twin Flame, your life is about to change. It may not be dramatic at first, in fact, it will probably be very subtle and maybe even completely unnoticeable. Making a choice changes everything. Your choices have tremendous power and you can use this power to create in your reality.

Right now, I'm going to show you how to attract your Twin Flame. Just as dependably as 2 + 2 = 4. You will attract your Twin Flame if you follow the steps precisely presented in this book. Attracting your Twin Flame can be easy, although you might be tempted to give up many times along the way. But if you do give up, you can always choose to get back on the horse by completing the *Attracting Your Twin Flame Meditation Exercise.*

It is time to continue on our Twin Flame journey together. This isn't "woo-woo," nor is this magic and make-believe, it's the simplest and most fundamental law of the Universe and it has been written about for ages. Yes, it is the *Law of Attraction* in action; the organizing principle of our Universe. I'm going to show you step by step exactly how to attract your Twin Flame. You will be taken from your decision, to meeting, all the way to KEEPING your Twin Flame for the rest of your life in Harmonious Twin Flame Union.

God told me 80 percent of all Twin Flame Unions break up before they make it through a lifetime together. This is because of the tremendous difficulty souls experience keeping such a powerful lover and teacher in their lives on Earth. I have decided with the utmost conviction to invest in my Twin Flame Union for life, and I will show you the tools I have so that you can create an unstoppable and permanent Harmonious Twin Flame Union too. People in any kind of relationship, even with their soul mate, can use these tools to create happy, healthy, and balanced relationships as well. It is up to you to use the tools as you desire. Without the tools I present to you, God's statistic tells me most people will likely not last in their Twin Flame Union for a lifetime. But with the right guidance, the right decisions, and the right tools, you CAN be with your Ultimate Lover for the rest of your eternal life. Don't believe me? That's fine. It's not necessary for you to believe without proof. But the only way for you to find out is to sincerely become an avid learner, and commit to the process I am showing you. You must only complete the steps. You don't need to believe the road to Phoenix will get you there from Los Angeles, you only need to drive it. Or walk it if you're crazy.

Be Present with what Arises

Things like this happen in your life so naturally and automatically that you probably won't even notice the difference. You don't need to realize it's happening for you to continue your Twin Flame journey. You do need to be present with what arises. You need to face, to be aware of, and to be present with whatever is happening in your life, and what's happening within you.

Imagine you did the *Attracting Your Twin Flame Meditation Exercise,* and a week later a new potential partner comes into your life.

Imagine for a moment this partner is absolutely not what you are looking for. You want your Twin Flame! You desire your Ultimate Lover. That's why you're reading this book. But Sam Schmoe comes walking along ready to sweep you off your feet for a few months, or a week, and then nothing. Nothing! How many times have you dated Sam? Three? Five? Plenty enough? I'm about to tell you to date Sam again even if Sam is clearly not your Twin Flame.

Here are the parameters within which I make my recommendation: If dating Sam again excites you, entices you, and enriches your life experience, then go for it. Date Sam Schmoe. Sam is the gateway to your Twin Flame. Sam is showing you something, beckoning you forth toward your desired Twin Flame reality. Sam is showing you what you need to do in order to attract your Twin Flame, and Sam is either going to fall away naturally to reveal the next step, or reveal themselves as your true Twin Flame in disguise! You may need to date Sam and clear the patterns existing within you to make it through to your Twin Flame. These are the patterns which prevent you from being physically with your Twin Flame right now. These are the steps you need to take in order to reveal your true Twin Flame.

One of your patterns might be attracting the same type of partner who abuses you and takes advantage of you, time and time again. One of your patterns might also be to find someone who looks and sounds perfect, but ends up being not what they seemed at first. Your pattern might even be running away from someone who is genuinely trying to connect and love you. Clear your patterns and you clear the path to your Twin Flame.

It is safe to date Sam, it is safe to explore with Sam, it is healthy and natural for you to move through your experience with Sam. Sam may not want the same things as you, but something about Sam is probably going to excite you, entice you, make you want to date them, and make you want to get to know them better. It is this enlivening energy which will cause you to want to connect with them, and it is this particular feeling which you need to follow in order to attract your Perfect Partner. This energy you feel, the same energy you feel when you choose to be with your Twin Flame, is going to appear and disappear throughout your life, time and time again. This is normal. This is the secret thread you need to follow. On the other end of this secret thread is your Ultimate Lover, your Twin Flame, and Perfect Love.

Don't go scrambling around looking for the feeling when it disappears. The secret thread will always lead you to your next step and only that. It almost always disappears when you reach the doorway and walk through it. Until it shows you the next door, your job is to continue working through whatever it led you to in the first place. It may be weeks, months, or years before it appears again, but you must be faithful to this feeling in order to find yourself at the doorway of your Twin Flame. Sam is just one common example of what happens when you choose your Twin Flame.

Lastly, it's important to continue to go within and do your spiritual work to find any and all blocks you have that are actually preventing you from finding and attracting your Twin Flame, as well as attaining Harmonious Union with them. You can call in your true Twin Flame over and over again, but if you are actually harboring great fear and resistance in meeting your Twin Flame and being with them, or feeling unworthy of them and their love for instance, then you are actually blocking the ability to meet them in the physical, or truly recognize them as your Twin Flame if this person has already been in your physical life in some way.

In the next chapter I teach you how to dissolve such blocks, and replace them with the truth of Love instead. This is the way to your Twin Flame in permanent Harmonious Union, and it's the key to your spiritual liberation of illusion to Union-Consciousness.

Chapter 5

The Mirror Exercise:
The Only Tool You Need

You're being taken on a journey through this book to your Twin Flame and Harmonious Union with them. Don't worry if you feel like you don't have any of the pieces put together yet, they are being carefully laid out for you in a very particular order. You're being shown just what you need in order to find and maintain permanent Harmonious Twin Flame Union with your Divine Counterpart.

I'm sharing with you my most powerful tool to help you attract your Twin Flame and keep them forever from Harmonious Union to Perfect Union. This one tool is so powerful, it can be used in any situation to help you create whatever it is you desire in your reality, but for the purpose of this book, we will direct it toward finding and maintaining your Twin Flame Union. This is a specific and scientific process I share that is as dependable and repeatable as the mathematical constant, pi ("π" = 3.14159), which is the ratio of the circumference of any circle to the diameter of that circle.

One of the primary purposes of the *Mirror Exercise* is to take back your power from anything that makes you unhappy, and actually realize that nothing outside of you can ever make you happy, yes, that even includes your Twin Flame. So, if it's true that nothing outside of you can make you happy, then there's something inside you blocking the happiness that naturally resides permanently within you. Your Twin Flame cannot make you happy. Only your relationship with God can create happiness. **Vibrating to Harmonious Union with God will naturally attract your Twin Flame into your life** (*hint, hint*). But to get to this place, we must begin creating opportunities to go inside ourselves and heal the blocks to our happiness and our Harmonious Twin Flame Union.

Between Shaleia and I, we have experienced and explored many different healing modalities from all over the world. Nothing has come close to the healing power of the *Mirror Exercise*. Meditation is a wonderful practice, but it's a very slow route alone in achieving enlightenment, especially if you are truly not an advanced expert meditator or do not have an enlightened spiritual teacher. If you combine the Mirror Exercise with meditation, yoga, prayer, or any other spiritual practices you have, you will greatly benefit and highly accelerate your spiritual progress. The Mirror Exercise does not conflict with any spiritual practices. It perfectly complements them, and it stands absolute and strong on its own as a primary spiritual practice. The Mirror Exercise is mine and Shaleia's most fundamental spiritual practice; our second is meditation, contemplation, and prayer; and thirdly, we do daily oracle card readings for ourselves with God. We have chosen these specific spiritual practices because they are best suited for our lifestyle and our individual and unique way of connecting and conversing with the Divine.

The reason why I say that the Mirror Exercise is more powerful than meditating your way to enlightenment, like many are taught, is because the Mirror Exercise is designed to go to all the places you are most uncomfortable inside of yourself and heal it with your awareness of love. In traditional meditation you don't have to go anywhere in your consciousness that you don't want to, or, go to places in your consciousness that you're not even aware of yet; but to have your Twin Flame, you must heal the core places in your consciousness that are upset and needing resolve and relief, specifically in the areas of unconditional and romantic love.

The Mirror Exercise: A New & Faster Method to Achieving Divine Union

This sacred practice of the *Mirror Exercise* can and will assist you all the way to your enlightenment, otherwise known as self-realization, or your ascension. This will be your natural next step once you attain your permanent Harmonious Twin Flame Union. The practice of Mirroring does not end until you enter Perfect Union (ascension/enlightenment) with the Divine and your Twin Flame. This will happen simultaneously in the same holy instant.

Doing the Mirror Exercise does get easier and easier with time. It is important you have a journal or notepad specifically to write down the Mirror Exercise while you are in the process of mastering it. We highly suggest this until you master the basics of the Mirror Exercise and release any and all resistance to doing this spiritual exercise. As you release resistance to doing the Mirror Exercise and become highly proficient in the basic steps, you will begin to learn how to do the Mirror Exercise automatically in your consciousness as upsets arise. As you reach this step, you may have to take time out to be alone and Mirror Exercise within yourself your upset(s), but as you become even more masterful, the "end-goal" is being able to Mirror Exercise your upsets and heal them fluidly, even as you are in the throes of experiencing an upset.

As you close the gap to your Harmonious Union with your Twin Flame, you will want to have the Mirror Exercise mastered to this point. This is because when your Twin Flame is behaving in a way that triggers you, as opposed to escalating into a fight or emotionally shutting down and distancing yourself, you will be able and spiritually mature enough to Mirror Exercise on the spot and heal your upset with your Twin Flame. As you do this with your Twin Flame, and also your other relationships (they are not excluded from you Mirror Exercising an upset they bring up in you), you are taking full responsibility for your feelings, emotions, and healing in whatever arises in your experience and within your consciousness. You are always responsible for mirroring whatever arises within you, no one else is responsible for your spiritual work or ever will be.

Your Twin Flame and your other relationships are not obligated to do the *Mirror Exercise* or heal an upset between you two. You alone are responsible for your happiness. **No one has power over you to make you feel _ANY_ way, whatsoever.** That is huge, I invite you to meditate on the power of my previous sentence, because if you do, you will ultimately realize how freeing that is for you and for other people and your relationships with them. You'll never desire to play "victim" again or enable others who are playing that same behavioral pattern, because the Truth is too powerful.

I've had people *live* to try to make me unhappy, and ultimately they were ejected from my experience because I only ever support the Divine in me and my relationships, and they either must choose to change themselves to match my vibration, or vibrate out of my reality.

With your Twin Flame there is a different set of rules than the rules of a non-Twin Flame relationship. This is because you are literally One at the core with your Twin Flame; as you choose love and healing through doing the Mirror Exercise, they experience that resulting unity within as well, and you'll begin to notice positive internal and external results with your Twin Flame Union. As you begin to notice clear signs that as you do the work to mirror your upsets and genuinely heal them, you experience the peace, relief, and togetherness you're desiring in your life, and with your Twin Flame.

I can't tell you how many times people in my *Twin Flame Ascension School* have used the Mirror Exercise to heal a communication block with their Twin Flame, and with gentle love, patience, and persistence, they are unblocked on social media by their Twin Flame! Or even how a student in mine and Shaleia's school devoted her life intensely to the *Mirror Exercise*, our teachings, and the support of our school and Facebook group (Twin Flames Universe: Open Forum), and actually arrived into her permanent Harmonious Twin Flame Union; and now her and her Twin Flame are teaching others how to do what we taught them, and what you are learning now in this book.

The thing with healing a block though is that you may have healed it, but then another layer to that block reveals itself. So don't be surprised or upset when you swore you healed an upset of being abandoned, for instance, and then you experience an upset with feeling abandoned later on again. This is a deep traumatic pain with many layers to it, but as you continue healing, the layers do peel off until it's fully resolved with only love remaining where you once felt hurt and emptiness. You cannot control your healing, you can only surrender and feel relief in handing it over completely to God. The promise of faith in God is that you will not be abandoned.

Choosing radical compassion for yourself, your Twin Flame, and others in the world is absolutely essential to vibrating to Harmonious Union Consciousness. It's never appropriate to beat yourself up for having an upset arise to the surface, especially if it's an upset you believe you already permanently healed. The correct posture is self-love and compassion, and return to doing the Mirror Exercise and go deeper in your self-loving. This love you are cultivating for yourself is a critical foundational pillar for your Harmonious Twin Flame Union, because what you are actively achieving is Divine unconditional love. Without choosing unconditional love for yourself, your Twin, and others, you will not be able to manifest Harmonious Union, because **Harmonious Union can only grow and bloom in the pristine soil of unconditional love.**

As you very much desire unconditional love and acceptance from your beloved Twin Flame, they very much desire that from you, but you must give it to yourself first and offer it to them when they are clearly putting a bid out toward you for unconditional love and acceptance. Sometimes your Twin Flame needs to experience a lesson in being with someone romantically while you're doing your Mirror Exercise and the spiritual work to be with them. This is one experience many are challenged in. Regardless of what's happening with your Twin Flame, are you going to love and trust your Twin Flame to experience their own spiritual lessons while simultaneously loving them unconditionally and accepting them? Or will you be angry, punishing, and try to control them? How you treat your Twin Flame is in direct relationship to how you treat yourself. If you choose to release control over your Twin Flame and their spiritual lessons, as well as release control in how they perceive you (many people try to put on a façade of "perfection"), you will experience your Twin Flame grow in attraction and appeal toward you because you are a beaming light of authenticity, unconditional love, and acceptance. Who doesn't find that attractive? Your Twin Flame is naturally attracted to your authenticity. Just you being you, and not you "photo-shopping" or controlling yourself, or your life experience. The *Mirror Exercise* is also designed for you to fall in love with your true authentic self, which automatically magnetizes your Twin Flame to you, and deepens your Harmonious Union once you achieve that.

The Mirror Exercise: All You Need to Attract and Attain Harmonious Twin Flame Union

Exactly how does the Mirror Exercise work in relationship to your consciousness? Your external experience is created within your internal consciousness. Your internal consciousness is based off your choices, thoughts, and feelings. This is because your thoughts and feelings arise from a core choice to feel good or bad, and subsequent thoughts and feelings are a result of that choice. Your life is not happening outside of you, your life is happening within you and expressing itself outward by magnetizing vibrational experiences to you. Even now as you read these words you are reading them within yourself using your vision, which is interpreted inside your brain; and how you think and feel regarding what you're reading is happening within you now and throughout your experience of the book. So when your Twin Flame, God, or other relationships you have are triggering you (that's what we call an "upset"), it's because they are mirroring a thought/belief you are having that is out of alignment with the Divine Mind, which is the consciousness of Heaven, and is your natural state of well-being. These upsets are showing you the way back Home if you actively choose your healing and your Harmonious Union with the Divine and yourself. This is why you can greatly accelerate on your spiritual journey using the sacred Mirror Exercise. Its very essence is designed to get you not just your Harmonious Twin Flame Union, but a clear and direct path back to your perfect internal state. You can even use the Mirror Exercise to heal physical ailments and sicknesses within yourself and others (and I have done so), but that is a topic for another book.

I am going to give you four examples in this chapter of how to utilize the Mirror Exercise. You use the Mirror Exercise whenever you are *upset*. Two of the examples will display upsetting interactions in the area of family and work, while the other two interactions will display the most common upsets people have with their Twin Flame. These two common upsets are:

1. **I'm upset at my Twin Flame because they're not communicating with me.**

2. **I'm upset at my Twin Flame because they do not want to be with me.**

Let's first begin this exercise with an easy example of a hypothetical upset you are having in the area of family. Imagine your sister constantly harasses you whenever you talk to her. You call her and she is harassing you. You show up at a family dinner and she's harassing you. You're eating a delicious sandwich on the boulevard with your good friend, and your sister sees you and begins harassing you. Why is she harassing you? It is because she loves you! I don't mean that she's harassing you because she loves you. I mean her Divine Self loves you so much that she's willing to mirror within you where it is you are misaligned within yourself. Technically, it's just God loving you through her in order for your pattern to be cleared. How is she mirroring something for you? She's reflecting back to you that within your consciousness you are harassing yourself in some way.

As you follow along with the provided examples, use your own personal story to complete the Mirror Exercise. What story should you use? **Anything that is upsetting you now**, and preferably something that is upsetting you the most. Typically in my Union with Shaleia, we will experience a handful of emotional and spiritual upsets coming to the surface to be released with one or more issues at a time. It's like a spiritual onion that falls away layer after layer and when it's healed is transformed into a beautiful lotus flower. We do not need to be in control of what comes to the surface to be healed at any particular time because the process is very natural and organic. Nothing occurs as we expect it, and that is a very, very good thing. It is from this place of patience and non-attachment that we can easily move through whatever arises within us in the moment, and trust what's releasing is in our best and highest interest, and in the highest interest of our Harmonious Twin Flame Union.

In your Harmonious and pre-Harmonious Twin Flame Union, many misaligned thoughts and beliefs based on separation consciousness are going to come to the surface of your consciousness for healing. You're going to need a specific, simple, and conscious process that can assist you through your challenges, or you're going to find you and your Twin Flame have developed the dreaded "Twin Flame Runner Dynamic." This is when both partners, on some level, run in the opposite direction of their Union. Notice how I left out the "chaser" part of what people believe to be the "runner/chaser dynamic?" This is because your Twin Flame is mirroring how you push yourself away somewhere within your consciousness. Running and chasing actually can only logically happen with a non-Twin Flame relationship. But if you're either running from or chasing your Twin Flame, it's because you are running away from yourself somewhere deep inside. Doing the Mirror Exercise on this upset will go deeper and resolve this issue completely.

When your Twin Flame upsets you, it's because your Twin Flame is reflecting something in you which is out of alignment with your Divine Self. Your Divine Self is the part of you which exists always as pure love and is also referred to as your Higher Self. So you're actually doing something to yourself within your consciousness to upset you, and that's actually why you're upset with someone else in the first place. The Mirror Exercise is a potent tool to address and clear these upsets from your reality, so you may not only experience greater peace, love, and happiness, but heal the core blocks preventing you directly from your Harmonious Twin Flame Union.

The Mirror Exercise:
STEP ONE

Write out one concise sentence of what exactly is upsetting you. Try to understand what exactly your core upset is when you write it down, so you're clear and succinct.

"My sister is upsetting me because she is always harassing me every time I talk with her!"

There are a few parts to this:

The *who* – my sister.
The *what* – she's upsetting me!
The *why* – because she's harassing me.
The *where/when* – every time I talk with her.

Now you have all the parts to Step One of the Mirror Exercise. Good job! If you didn't quite get it for your story yet, we can imagine an upset with Riley your co-worker in order to assist you further with your clarity. Imagine while working with Riley for a few months, you begin experiencing Riley not giving as much to your working relationship. Riley expects you to give more to your job than Riley does, so you essentially have to pick up the slack at work, and you are expected by your employer to continue giving either the same amount of energy or more. So, on a piece of paper you would write:

> *"Riley is upsetting me because he/she expects me to give more at work and our working relationship than the support I receive back from him/her."*

What are the parts?

> The ***who*** – Riley.
> The ***what*** – is upsetting me.
> The ***why*** – because he/she expects me to give more than what I receive from him/her.
> The ***where/when*** – in our relationship at work.

Now, let's do Step One of the Mirror Exercise for the two most common upsets people have with their Twin Flame. There are many different variations of the same upsets I am providing in these two examples, so you can actually use precisely the same examples below if they are your core upsets with your Twin Flame, and/or you can alter them to express a specific upset you are having that is either similar or different to the examples provided below.

"I'm upset at my Twin Flame because they're not communicating with me on social media/email/phone, etc."

The **who** – my Twin Flame.
The **what** – is upsetting me.
The **why** – because they're not communicating with me.
The **where/when** – on social media/email/phone, etc.

"I'm upset at my Twin Flame because they do not want to be with me or have anything to do with my life. I'm upset because I feel abandoned and betrayed by my Twin Flame."

The **who** – my Twin Flame.
The **what** – is upsetting me.
The **why** – because they do not want to be with me and I feel abandoned and betrayed because of it.
The **where/when** – in my/our life.

In review of Step One: Write out in one concise sentence the upset you are experiencing. Do your best to identify the root of your upset toward the person. This piece is important in getting clear about the deeper upset within you that's ultimately a core block and upset to your Harmonious Twin Flame Union. Healing this upset means you are one step closer to your Union!

The Mirror Exercise:
STEP TWO

Write the sentence from Step One all over again, but *switch all the nouns to pronouns* and point them to yourself. For instance:

Example A:

STEP ONE: "My sister is upsetting me because she is always harassing me every time I talk with her!"

STEP TWO: "I am upsetting myself because I am always harassing myself every time I talk to myself!"

Example B:

STEP ONE: "Riley is upsetting me because he/she expects me to give more to our working relationship than what I receive from him/her."

STEP TWO: "I am upsetting myself because I expect myself to give more to my relationship than what I receive from myself."

Example C:

STEP ONE: "I'm upset at my Twin Flame because they're not communicating with me on social media/email/phone, etc."

STEP TWO: "I'm upset at myself because I am not communicating with myself."

Example D:

STEP ONE: "I'm upset at my Twin Flame because they do not want to be with me or have anything to do with my life. I'm upset because I feel abandoned and betrayed by my Twin Flame."

STEP TWO: "I'm upset at myself because I do not want to be with myself or have anything to do with myself. I'm upset at myself because I feel abandoned and betrayed by myself."

The Mirror Exercise works because your external life is always a reflection of all levels of your consciousness, which is created by the core choices inside your mind. What you're choosing on the inside of yourself is what is being created on the outside of yourself. That's the result and the truth of the Law of Attraction. As within, so without. These annoyances or upsets are annoyances or upsets *inside of you*. You're automatically creating on the outside which is being reflected back to you from inside yourself.

The harassing sister? Yes, in this example she's reflecting back to you how you're harassing yourself. Each reflection is totally personal and never universal between the same experiences and people. Only you can determine the out of alignment thoughts, feelings, and beliefs you are holding on the inside which are causing your upsets.

The co-worker relationship issue with Riley? In this example, Riley is reflecting back to you how you're not giving to yourself, and how you're expecting yourself to give more in relationships than you give to yourself, so you actually have nothing to give to your relationships until you choose to start giving to yourself. Perhaps giving to yourself in this example would be a loving and firm boundary as to what you will and will not do. This is how you start cultivating self-respect and self-trust, and teaching others how to appropriately treat you in every circumstance.

Your Twin Flame who won't talk to you? They are mirroring back to you directly how you are not communicating with an aspect of yourself. You might think to yourself, "What does that mean? How am I not communicating with myself?" Well, perhaps you ignore your needs, you ignore your intuition, you ignore putting up a healthy boundary with yourself and others, you ignore listening to yourself, you ignore your sexuality & sexual needs, your creativity, your spirituality, your divine guidance & signs that come through you and other people and situations, your beauty, intelligence and power, your inner child, you ignore what your finances are telling you; *you are ignoring being with your Divine Self and cultivating a real loving relationship with yourself.* The list of how you potentially avoid and neglect yourself could go on, but you get the picture. Somewhere inside of you, you are not talking to yourself: your Divine Self. But you can heal this one by choosing to no longer ignore your Divine Self in any way, but choose to listen to yourself and develop a better self-relationship, so you no longer experience this upset continuing, or your beloved Twin Flame not talking to you.

Your Twin Flame doesn't want to be with you? In this example your Twin Flame is mirroring how you don't want to be with yourself. Perhaps you're trying to *get* something from someone outside of yourself. Yes, this certainly includes your Twin Flame, because you don't want to get love from yourself or from God within you. You try and get it from your Twin Flame and so they push you away. You are naturally magnetic to your Twin Flame only when you are complete within yourself, rather than coming from a needy state which is a repulsive energy. You are fulfilled only by and through God's Divine Love. The instant you "need" something to fulfill you, you are engaging in co-dependent behavior and are looking to your Twin Flame as Source, rather than God as your Source. Your Twin Flame can never replace the role of God and God's Love for you. Many would like to treat their Twin Flame like this but it's an inappropriate role to place them in because they are not your Creator. They can never come from the experience or truth of loving you from a place of having created you in perfect Divinity and Love.

There are many other examples of how you do not want to be with yourself because you are uncomfortable being alone with yourself and your Divine Self, but this is the opportunity provided to truly become your real best friend above anyone else aside from God. Your Twin Flame is your best friend, but God is your best friend first, then you, THEN your Twin Flame. This is the *proper order* of relationship. You'll notice though that being your own best friend is practically the same as God being your best friend, and your Twin Flame naturally is and becomes your best friend as a result of your above priorities.

When you do not want to be with yourself, or with God, you experience abandonment, which also feels like betrayal, because it is.

God could never ever abandon you. If God created abandonment then it would be real, but it's an illusion because God only creates perfection, and we are One with our beloved Creator. When you don't want to be with yourself, you abandon yourself and thus open yourself up to the experience of being abandoned by others (this is how mirroring works). But if you open up your Divine Logic, you will see as I have seen, that you cannot be abandoned by someone who never truly claimed you as theirs. So, you were never abandoned because you were never claimed by them in the first place, you just experienced the illusion based on belief that you were claimed in love by them. People who abandon their relationships also practice self-abandonment, or else they would be incapable of the act. So, just feel compassion for them and others when you realize this. When you choose to stop abandoning yourself and start listening to yourself and loving yourself where you need to, you cease self-abandonment and develop self-trust, love, and confidence. As a result, your Twin Flame will change their tune about not wanting to be with you, because in claiming yourself, you claim ALL of you, which naturally includes your Twin Flame because they are you too.

Notice how example C and D are so inter-connected? That's because the two upsets are practically the same upset at the core. There are lots of clues there as to how you might be abandoning yourself and how to heal it.

The Mirror Exercise:
STEP THREE

Now ask yourself, "Is there ANY truth to this statement?" The answer is always "Yes" because it's in your experience. Go deeper until you find the root of the issue if you like. But as the famous Buddha once said, "Just pull the thorn out and move on. Do not look at it." This is because if we psycho-analyze every detail of where an upset originated from we lose focus on just going in and loving that part of ourselves calling for love, and over-analyzing an upset is a form of control and avoidance to doing Step Four. Just love yourself by doing Step Four, and move on to healing the next upset which arises.

Let's apply this to the upset of example A:

> *"I am upsetting myself because I am always harassing myself every time I talk to myself!"*

Now sincerely ask yourself if there is ANY truth to this statement. Take your time and contemplate how it might be true in your consciousness. Could I be harassing myself? Under what circumstances do I harass myself? Your answer may look something like this:

"Yes, I do harass myself. I notice any time I am speaking to myself in my head, I am saying negative things to myself, and I believe I'm not perfect in some or all ways. I suppose if anyone else said these things to me, I would feel harassed by them. I'm also sure that if I ever said these things to anyone else, they would feel harassed and pressured by me. So yes, this statement is very true for me." *(Hint: remember the answer is always "Yes").*

Let's continue with example B:

"I am upsetting myself because I expect myself to give more into my relationship than what I receive from myself."

Is there any truth to this statement?

"Yes. I am not giving myself what I need, and I expect myself to give more into my relationships than I am able to. I do this because I hope that I can get from my relationships what I am choosing to not give to myself. I know I can heal my cycle of co-dependent behaviors, because I know God is my source of healing and happiness, not other people."

That's the reason Riley's behavior upsets you so much. Riley is reflecting in you the misaligned part of you that doesn't give yourself what you need! Your upset has nothing to do with Riley at all, you are only upset by what *you are doing to yourself within your own consciousness!*

Your upset with yourself is the reason you're experiencing Riley as your co-worker right now, and they're helping you heal a core block to your Twin Flame Union! Work through these issues within yourself as Riley presents them to you as a reflection from within yourself, and Riley will naturally fall away (or align with your new vibration); allowing the next step toward your Twin Flame and Harmonious Union to unfold. It doesn't have to be Riley, your Twin Flame, or your sibling who will be presenting you with issues and challenges. The people around you, even someone in passing can cause you to feel upset. It is your job as you move toward your Ultimate Lover to clear these patterns, so that you may clear the way to your Harmonious Twin Flame Union, and permanently maintain your Harmonious Union. Doing the Mirror Exercise is an activity that does not stop until you attain Perfect Union (I discuss more in depth Perfect Union in a later chapter).

Moving on to example C:

> *"I'm upset at myself because I am not communicating with myself."*

Is there any truth to this statement?

"Yes. I am not communicating with my Authentic Self. I believe if I express who I truly am inside I will be rejected by my Twin Flame. I know that rejecting my Authentic Self is abandoning who I am inside, but I'm not sure how to feel safe being myself around others and especially my Twin Flame."

Once again, you can see your upset has actually nothing to personally do with your Twin Flame, but everything to do with you. You cannot control how others perceive, experience, or react to you. It's not even your job to care. It's your job to only express the authentic love and creative expression you are. Your Twin Flame pushing you away is only an opportunity for you to go deeper in loving who you are at your core, and not to control how you appear or are to your Twin Flame. Controlling how you appear or are creates blocks to intimacy with your Twin Flame because you are blocking being intimate with yourself.

Lastly, let's look at example D:

> *"I'm upset at myself because I do not want to be with myself or have anything to do with my life. I'm upset at myself because I feel abandoned and betrayed by myself."*

"Yes, it's true. I struggle being able to be in my company with God and my Divine Self for long, if at all. I am not 100 percent happy with my life so I numb out and create ways to escape what I don't like about myself and my life. I notice I abandon and betray myself because I do not listen to myself, but I'll listen to what others want from me and act based off of them and their wants and needs regarding me and my life."

As you can see, your Twin Flame is loving you totally by showing you your core misaligned thoughts and actions you are having out of step with your Harmonious Twin Flame Union. If you cannot be in your own company, the company of your Divine Self, and listen and act accordingly to your Divine Self, you cannot be in the presence of your Twin Flame long, if at all, because once again, they are One with you. How can you be long in the presence of your Twin Flame if you can barely stand being in the presence of your Authentic and Divine Self? It doesn't work and your Twin Flame mirrors that for you. Harmonious Twin Flame Union is a Divine Love and that is why we are teaching you how to align with it in order to permanently have your Harmonious Union. Once again, it's not about you "being perfect." You already are perfection. This is about clearing out only the core blocks of love to your Harmonious Twin Flame Union, and as you apply this exercise and our teachings in this book and experience the subsequent positive results of that, you will feel encouraged to keep going. To have your Harmonious Twin Flame Union you must commit to the spiritual work and process we share with you and go all in. Only going half in to this work will only give you half-in results. Going all in will provide you with all-in results. You have nothing to lose, and only everything Divine to gain.

When you finally meet your Twin Flame, you're going to run into so many little issues like the example upsets we share that have the potential to throw you and your Twin Flame hurling off in opposite directions. It's not worth it though. It's not worth losing your Twin Flame over these little upsets. Just do the exercise and the upsets will be a simple matter to resolve. If you choose to not do the Mirror Exercise, then these little upsets could ruin your chances of Harmonious Union with your most Perfect Lover. Don't let this one slip by. You can't afford to! Skip any part of the book other than the *Mirror Exercise.* Don't skip this one thing. You owe it to yourself and your Twin Flame to learn this material and use it. You can't attain your Harmonious Twin Flame Union without it. Trust me, because this is the process that attained my success and the success of other couples in my Twin Flame Ascension School, who ultimately achieved Harmonious Union with their Twin Flame.

If you choose to do this work, you are among the few who will attract and *KEEP* your Harmonious Twin Flame Union for eternal life. The Mirror Exercise still blows my mind every time I do it. But I do it, and it works to heal my core blocks to my beloved every time, even if it's hard for me to look at. If it works, it is real, and if it is real, it works. You don't even need to understand how or why it works to fully complete the process. I invite you to complete the process and you will reap the rewards and benefits all the way along. A major benefit of the reward is true inner peace, happiness, and deeper levels of loving with your Twin Flame whether you've met them yet or not.

Let's go over the steps we've covered so far:

STEP ONE: Write out in one concise sentence the upset you are experiencing.

STEP TWO: Write the sentence all over again, but switch all the nouns to pronouns so they point to yourself.

STEP THREE: Ask yourself, "Is there ANY truth to this statement?" and go deeper until you find the root of the issue, but you are intelligent and a spiritual genius so you already know the answer is "Yes," because that's what you're experiencing as a result of your experience and consciousness.

You will need to write this exercise down as you do it. My spiritual teacher stressed this so many times with me and she was right. Magic happened every time I wrote it down in Step One, then wrote it down again in Step Two when I flipped the words around to point to myself. This is the best way to learn it and commit to this as your new spiritual practice to bring you your Permanent Harmonious Twin Flame Union. Eventually, you will be mastered enough to do it in your head anywhere you go, but you can't get there until you become comfortable with the process by writing it on a notepad or a special journal first.

The Mirror Exercise:
STEP FOUR

Speak to the inner part of yourself which is causing the problem and love yourself.

This is where the healing takes place and where your harassing sister, or your Twin Flame who ghosted you no longer bothers you. When you no longer experience the upset in your reality and you experience relief in your vibration, it is clear you have actually healed it. If it continues to come up again, and again, and again, keep doing the Mirror Exercise until you actually discover the root of the issue and heal it. Sometimes the healing occurs in layers. When you have finally healed it, it will not come up in your experience again. **When your sister's harassment genuinely stops upsetting you, or it stops altogether, you have completed healing this aspect of yourself.** It is eerie how it works, and it is amazing the results you can reap by doing your inner work.

So let's look at the sentence of Step Two again:

"I am upsetting myself because I am always harassing myself every time I talk to myself."

We're going to go and speak with the part of ourselves which is, in this example, harassing the rest of us. Let's have an imaginary dialogue. In order to do this, we need to be able to face, and listen to the part of ourselves which is causing the problem. So, we center into ourselves and speak to the energy within us that is feeling the upset.

"Hi, why are you harassing me?"
The reply is, "Well, because you aren't beautiful, perfect, and good."

You instinctively say back while knowing the truth, "I know I am beautiful, perfect, and good in the eyes of God."

You have now already begun giving yourself love where there was a lack of love. After this, wait and see if you hear anything back. Sometimes this could be the end of it. You have declared you are beautiful, perfect, and good to the part which previously believed otherwise, perhaps that's all you needed to do. The problem is then resolved only through your self-love. But, perhaps you hear something back like, "No, you're not perfect. When you were five your mother told you to brush your hair so you would look good, but you went to the birthday party that day without brushing your hair. You're not perfect so you can't be lovable."

In this case, you might go speak with the hurt child inside of yourself, and remind her or him that she or he is very lovable and absolutely beautiful, divinely perfect, and good. You might hug the child, and send them love by bringing them into the deepest center of your heart.

You only need to find the source of the place within you which is not loving and give it the love it is calling for.

After that, the person inside you who says you are not beautiful, Divinely perfect, or good will be integrated into your whole self, and your experience of being upset when your sister tries harassing you will no longer occur because you know the truth of yourself. She may even stop harassing you altogether because there's no longer a button to push. This exercise works like magic. You will want to get the hang of this before you meet your Twin Flame, because upsets will come quickly and powerfully when you're with your Twin. The reason Twin Flame energy is more powerful, is because Twin Flame energy is highly amplified compared to the energy between soul mates or romantic relationships; this is due to them being your most perfect and clear mirror of your thoughts, feelings, and choices.

Let's do the example with Riley as well to help bring more clarity to this exercise:

STEP ONE: Write out in a concise sentence the upset you are experiencing:

> **"Riley is upsetting me because he/she expects me to give more to our working relationship than what I receive from him/her."**

STEP TWO: Write the sentence all over again, but switch all the nouns to pronouns and point them to yourself:

"I am upsetting myself because I expect myself to give more into my relationship than what I receive from myself."

STEP THREE: Ask yourself, "Is there ANY truth to this statement?" and go deeper if necessary until you find the root of the issue:

"Yes, this is true because I am not giving myself what I need, and I expect myself to give more into my relationships than I am able to. I do this because I hope that I can get from my relationships what I am not giving myself already."

STEP FOUR: Speak to the part of yourself which is causing the problem and love yourself:

Close your eyes and imagine the misaligned part of yourself standing near you. "Why do you hope you can get more from your relationships than what you are not giving to yourself already?" you might say to it.

"Because I don't want to be loved. I want to avoid being loved because I don't deserve love," it might respond.

"Oh, but you do deserve love!" you might say, pausing to listen for any further response. If you experience no deeper issue arising, you can then ask that part of yourself what it needs to feel deserving of love.

"I need to be held and told that I deserve love," it might say.

It will always tell you what it needs to feel loved. All you need to do now is give that part of yourself exactly what it told you it needed in order to feel deserving of love. Just do it in your imagination. Hold that part of yourself in your imagination and tell it it deserves love. Once you feel that part of you has been loved completely, you are finished with the Mirror Exercise. One of the psychological and physiological benefits of the visualization step of the Mirror Exercise is that *it's been scientifically proven that the brain does not know the difference between what you see and experience in the physical world, and what you see and experience when you utilize your visualization and imaginative faculties.*

The deep truth of this science actually has a major impact on your health and healing, because you can literally "go back in time" and heal your childhood by giving to yourself what you didn't have back then. Your brain and consciousness will react like your perfect childhood happened (because you are giving yourself your perfect childhood), and healing will occur because the synaptic pathways in your brain will begin to rewire toward positivity, happiness, and well-being rather than depression, anxiety, and other mental and psychological imbalances. Shaleia specifically focused on healing her childhood when she went back "in time" in her mind and healed not being breast-fed by her mother or held enough as a baby and toddler. She visualized, and subsequently experienced, being a baby whose needs were perfectly attended to; she visualized being perfectly loved, held, and breast-fed by Divine Mother. Shaleia realized not having these core bonding experiences with her parents impacted her throughout her life and all the way up into her adulthood. She no longer experiences those negative consequences because of the powerful visualization step in the Mirror Exercise. In Shaleia's mind, she had a wonderful childhood and no longer experiences upsets as a result of not getting her needs met by her biological parents when she was a baby and child. When your childhood is fully healed, you are then able to step into exploring and experiencing your true adulthood.

Going back to what I mentioned earlier, you can know for certain that you have completed your healing when you no longer experience Riley's lousy work expectations upsetting you. If you are still having trouble completing Step Four, or need a little boost to your loving, then try adding the following visualization exercise to finish off this step.

Visualization Exercise for the Mirror Exercise: Step Four Point One

Close your eyes and imagine meeting the part of you which is not feeling loved, which you have identified to have been creating the issue which has arisen. Invite it to come closer to you, then invite it into a hug. Hug that part of you with an open heart, bringing that part of yourself deep into a loving hug. Tell that part of you how much you love it and pull it in even closer into you. If they haven't completely melted into you and become part of you, give them more love. Choose to love the part of you calling for love wholly.

The prescription is always more love. Love that part of you ten times more, a hundred times more, a trillion times more. You can even imagine a white or colorful light beaming from your heart center, and enveloping them with your perfect loving light. Your subconscious mind is going to do all the work for you if you choose to visualize and love this part of you that is out of alignment with love. Once you sense this part of you is loved and integrated and relieved in peace, you are complete.

The Mirror Exercise Steps

STEP ONE: Describe in one concise sentence the upset you are experiencing.

STEP TWO: Write the sentence all over again, but switch all the nouns to pronouns to point to yourself.

STEP THREE: Ask yourself, "Is there ANY truth to this statement?" The answer is always "Yes."

STEP FOUR: Speak to the part of yourself causing the upset and love yourself until you experience peace, relief, and completion within. Do the visualization exercise to further this healing if need be.

The Mirror Exercise: Final Thoughts

The Mirror Exercise is a powerful tool for attracting your Twin Flame and attaining permanent Harmonious Twin Flame Union. It's powerful because it brings you a new completion of a lesson or challenge, which is one step closer to your Twin Flame and Harmonious Union. This is because it clears the blocks that are not allowing you to raise your vibration to match the energy of Harmonious Twin Flame Union, and experience deeper levels of loving. When you choose your Twin Flame (as you have in the *Attracting Your Twin Flame Meditation Exercise*), you're starting on your Twin Flame journey to permanent Harmonious Twin Flame Union.

When you make a choice, the power of your choice immediately begins bringing you exactly what you asked for. You can use the power of your choice to attract anything. In this case, we're going step by step toward your Twin Flame in Harmonious Union. When you choose to be with your Twin Flame, everything you need to attract your Twin Flame will come to you at the perfect pace for you, and resources will be made available as you claim your support to Harmonious Union. Sometimes, you will experience challenges that cause you to feel upset. When you feel upset in any way, do the *Mirror Exercise* to clear the upset. If you're anything like me, you will not likely believe the upset is about anything but someone else. But, if you're willing to suspend your logical judgment and go deeper, simply do the exercise while you're upset, and you will find that it is effective in healing your upset on a deep internal level and usually at the root cause. Make it a habit in your relationship, Union, or life experience to step out for a few minutes every time you notice yourself getting upset. Shaleia and I regularly take breaks from arguments to go and do the Mirror Exercise. Often times, when we come back to each other, there is no longer anything to argue about, and we experience better communication, togetherness, and deeper authentic intimacy. If there isn't, we do the Mirror Exercise until we do.

If you are experiencing something you know is out of alignment with your Divine Self, but you do not believe you feel an upset, then it is highly likely you are numbed out to it. A woman came to me recently saying her partner was abusing her, but she didn't feel upset about it, this awareness allowed me to indicate to her how numbed out she was when it came down to experiencing abuse. I explained to her that she is safe to feel her feelings, and to acknowledge her upset at being abused. I then helped her identify her core upset, which is, being upset at herself for abusing herself. She was then able to do the last two steps of the Mirror Exercise, and she thanked me gratefully for helping her heal her long-standing history of abuse in relationships.

With each completion of the Mirror Exercise and with each upset healed, you bring yourself one step closer to your Twin Flame and Harmonious Union. Don't worry if you don't understand how to do it the first several times through. Just keep repeating the exercise until you understand how to do it, and get into the flow of it. It's absolutely and unequivocally essential if you're serious about maintaining your eternal Twin Flame Union in perfect harmony. You'll quickly realize why the Mirror Exercise is important to practice in your Union if you desire to maintain it as you enter and grow closer to your Twin Flame. In fact, you'll realize and appreciate how wonderful this tool is throughout your journey of being in Harmonious Union, and into Perfect Union together. Ultimately, making the decision to master the Mirror Exercise will change the way you experience your reality, and it will empower you to master consciously creating every aspect of your life, which includes you and your Twin Flame in Permanent Harmonious Union.

Ultimately, you will begin doing the Mirror Exercise by writing it out countless times, and I encourage this for quite some time until you feel the mastery of knowing and completing this on the inside, and you realize writing it down doesn't serve your process anymore. You will step up eventually to where you can do the process in your head, reversing the nouns around, and then loving yourself. When you are completely mastered in the *Mirror Exercise* you won't need to go through the steps anymore; you will discover that you recognize an upset in your reality, immediately **feel** into it within your own consciousness, and then **naturally give yourself the love you need.** The Mirror Exercise turns into a meditation, something you can organically and fluidly do in your daily life, but which will always require your conscious attention and specific focus.

Do not be fooled or overly ambitious into thinking you can immediately jump directly to mastery, because you must be patient and work to master the basic process first. Mastering the process means you have the correct inner foundation upon which to stand and move you forward to your goal properly. You can only achieve your Permanent Harmonious Twin Flame Union if you have a **high willingness to learn and a high willingness to change.** This is the correct disposition and qualities every true and committed spiritual student has, and this is a lesson everyone must learn. You must learn the steps by writing them down. You must learn the feeling process. You must learn how to identify upsets within your own consciousness. You must learn the absolute precision of *writing down* the steps the Mirror Exercise gives and requires of you. And when you do this, know you will eventually be able to do it with maximal ease and efficiency anywhere you are in your daily life because you have attained mastery there.

Chapter 6

Harmonious Twin Flame Union: Keeping Your Twin Flame for Life

How many Disney movies are about finding True Love? Walt Disney knew something genuine when he made all those movies, which continue to inspire so many people with hope for their own One True Love. He knew True Love was real. The movies didn't show you how to get True Love, only that it exists. You are being shown how to in this book. Your True Love is real, and your True Love is waiting just around the corner for you to make the decision to be united, and follow your feelings to be with them permanently. This is truly the first and last time you get to fall in love, and the love between you and your Twin Flame continues to deepen and expand for all of eternity. It is an incredible relief to finally have this aspect of your life handled forever.

Your Twin Flame doesn't need to make any decisions to come to you, but as Shaleia and I found out, we were making all the same decisions to come to each other at the same time because we are One at the core. We are so intrinsically connected, that our choices powerfully impact the choices of our Twin Flame. Your Twin Flame is connected to you always, you can feel them in your heart right now if you pause and choose to feel them there energetically. That person IS the longing you are feeling, that person IS the lover you seek day after day, moment after moment. That person IS real, and IS the appropriate lover to fulfill all you desire to have in a romantic connection and life partnership. This is more than having a "5D connection and affair," but actually bridging that separation to having a very real physical relationship, as you're naturally created to be.

I spent a significant amount of time writing down all the desires I had for a woman. I once joked with myself when writing this Love List that I would literally need a dozen women to fulfill even most of what I wanted from a woman on this list. But guess what? Shaleia is *everything* on my list and so much more. You deserve and have a partner that completes you in every way. You deserve and have a lover who will fulfill and satisfy your every need and desire, and then some. You deserve and have been created with your Perfect Partner, and you will attain them if you follow the steps being shown to you here.

Yes, you absolutely must make the decision. Do the *Attracting Your Twin Flame Meditation Exercise* if you want to find your Twin Flame. Yes, you absolutely must follow your feelings and move toward them, and you must have the ability to clean up any misaligned thoughts and beliefs causing upset within you using the Mirror Exercise. The Mirror Exercise will assist you in clearing any blocks and barriers you have within you, which are preventing you from being with your Twin Flame. This is key.

Stages of a Harmonious Twin Flame Union (Channeled)

When you meet your Twin Flame, you will find that clear and specific stages are occurring within your Union. There are four stages of a Twin Flame Union, and each with its own unique characteristics and experiences. No Union will ever have a clear stepping stone from one stage to the next because it is fluid. One part of your Union may be in Stage Two, while another part may be in Stage Four. It's all dependent upon how quickly you choose to move through the stages. The more you and your Twin Flame choose to work on your Union, the more quickly you will pass through these stages and inevitably find yourself completely in love in Harmonious Twin Flame Union. These stages occur all throughout Harmonious Twin Flame Union until you attain Perfect Union with your Twin Flame. This is because these stages, including the Mirror Exercise, are designed to continue purifying you until you ascend to Perfect Union with the Divine and your Twin Flame. You cannot prevent these changes from happening once you get into your Harmonious Twin Flame Union, but you can slow down the process significantly.

Stage One: The Decision

After you decide to be with your Twin Flame, you have already acquired them on the inside. This is no mistake. You are instantly bound to your Twin Flame in a very Earthly, real, and material way when you make the decision. You do not need to worry about whether they are on the planet, or married, or your age, or color. If you are deciding to be with your Twin Flame, they are deciding to be with you too. You will also find when your Twin Flame arrives, all things which matter to you on Earth are acceptable to you, because it's perfect and appropriate in your Union as lovers.

Making a decision is important because it aligns you to your Twin Flame. You need to decide on anything to move toward it, this is the Nature of how you are created, and it is the Nature of the Universe. Decision is the most important step. Everything else occurs as a result of your firm decision. You will also notice there is no stage before decision, there is nothing before you make a decision. It is only when you decide that anything can manifest for you. The decision stage is also one of trial and effort. You will be tried for your alignment with your Twin Flame. You will not be able to see, hear, feel, taste, or touch your Twin Flame until you work yourself into alignment with your Twin Flame, and Harmonious Twin Flame Union.

There is nothing you need to do other than the trials that appear before you: a waitress who is late with the bill before your pending flight, a car in front of you on your way to an appointment, a co-worker who upsets you regularly. You will need to pass all of these tests by remembering your true nature as a Divine Being and maintaining your high vibration. You will need to remember you are love, you are peace, you are safe, you are one with All That Is. This is how you honor your Divine Self. Follow your feelings and *feel* your feelings when it comes to the trials that arise. You will immediately sense a light and positive feeling when you make the choice to be with your Twin Flame. Follow that feeling wherever you find it, and you will eventually experience a reality filled with that feeling.

It is important to follow your heart in the direction of your highest dreams and desires. When you listen to the Divine Intuition within you and take your guided action steps, you literally get to live in the permanent reality of your dreams. Nothing can stop you from achieving your perfect love life, only you do. Your heart is naturally programmed to know the way Home to God and to your Twin Flame. Listen and follow the steps to love's all-encompassing embrace.

Following your intuitive feelings may seem like a high spiritual accomplishment, but it is normal for you. It is normal and natural for you to feel safe, to feel love, to feel at peace, to feel connected with everything. It is easy to achieve these things on a moment to moment basis, because this is your True Nature. It is easier for you to experience peace than it is to experience upset, because peace is your natural state of Being.

Work through the Mirror Exercise that Jeff and Shaleia have shown you, and you will find relief from your upsets quickly and efficiently, and clear blocks to your Harmonious Twin Flame Union. There is no quicker way yet shown to humanity to clear upsets than the Mirror Exercise as explained in the previous chapter. Your decisions will bring you what you decide to attain, every time. But each time, you must also bring yourself into alignment with what you desire.

Stage Two: Meeting

In every manifestation there is the receiving aspect. You ask for what you desire, you become aligned with what you desire, then you get what you desire every time, without exception. In manifesting your Twin Flame and Harmonious Union with them, there will come a time when you meet them. It will happen for you if you make the decision, and work through the situations, upsets, and circumstances which arise to bring you your desire.

Meeting is a stage, because it takes a long time for you to meet your Twin Flame on every level, because you are meeting *yourself* on every level of your Being. It took six months of daily contact before Jeff and Shaleia had completed their meeting stage. This stage is where all parts of you are becoming intimately acquainted with all parts of your Twin Flame on every level possible. The meeting stage will often take longer than six months for many Twin Flames who are not consciously focusing on developing their Union as efficiently as possible and for the purpose of Harmonious Twin Flame Union. Jeff and Shaleia are exceptional in the speed with which they developed their permanent and Harmonious Twin Flame Union. Most Unions will take three to five years to fully complete this stage. Stages can overlap and occur simultaneously, as Jeff and Shaleia found out. The third stage of "Upset" started to occur almost immediately into their Union.

Stage Three: Upset

There is no better title to describe the experience of the third stage in your Twin Flame Union. "Upset" is most fitting because this is what you will experience a majority of time in this stage and be presented with before and during Harmonious Twin Flame Union. There is no more important stage for you to pass through in this lifetime in keeping your Twin Flame. Your Twin Flame upsets you because they love you. Your Twin Flame is experiencing upset because you love them. You're not deliberately upsetting your Twin Flame, and they are not deliberately upsetting you, because you are each responsible for your own happiness and peace. Your Twin Flame is holding a space of love in their vibration, and wherever you are not holding that space for yourself, you are going to experience an upset until you love yourself in that area.

Don't worry, this process is designed to be workable for you. You will not experience all your upsets at once. You will experience a constant deepening of love and intimacy as you are working through all your upsets with the Mirror Exercise. As your love for each other and yourselves grow, you will experience deeper and more subtle upsets coming to the surface to be loved and healed. Once you get the hang of this process, you can almost time when your next cycle of upsets will be. Jeff and Shaleia noticed this like clockwork, and were able to anticipate the next wave, and the next wave of upset. They chose to create spaces of breaks naturally between their upsets, as they worked through this stage, knowing intuitively what stage was awaiting them next. As Jeff and Shaleia learned, it's important not to judge upsets as they arise, but to love and embrace them with compassion because this is what you're healing and it's the correct attitude toward your healing and your Twin Flame's healing. Naturally, your Twin Flame is your perfect reflection and mirror of your shared consciousness together. This is one of the gifts your Twin Flame brings to you and is a blessing, because they have the ability to see and to help you be your highest potential of Divine Expression.

Stage Four: Unconditional Love

Unconditional love is what you will be experiencing in the fourth stage of your Harmonious Twin Flame Union. Love is absolutely the result of deciding, working through the misalignment, and then receiving the fruits of removing the obstacles of love between you and your Twin Flame. You will, with absolute certainty, experience True Divine Love in this fourth stage of your Harmonious Twin Flame Union. The third stage of a Twin Flame Union usually takes the longest of any previous stage, but with each successfully realigned thought, with each newly loved part of you, you bring one part of yourself through to stage Four, which is a magnetic attractive field to your Twin Flame. You can't attain your Harmonious Twin Flame Union without continuing this process of unconditional love and acceptance.

These stages are sequential, but they are not linear. You will not find that one day you are completely in Upset, and the next you are completely in Love. There can be parts of you which are in Meeting, parts of you which are in Upset, and parts of you which are in Love *all in the same moment.* In time, all parts of the both of you will align into Love, and you will experience the fullest magnificence of your true Harmonious Twin Flame Union with your Ultimate Lover.

Unstoppable Unions

So many of us experience soul mate relationship attraction, and equate that to the best that love is ever going to get for us. We think, believe, see, and experience a love that starts off hot! – then diminishes over time. We think the best lover is going to be the one who has the hottest start, and sticks around long enough for us to get into a marriage with them. Many marriages today will end in divorce, but it doesn't have to be this way. You never need to settle on a relationship because you believe your Twin Flame is not going to enter your life, or choose to enter your life permanently. Having your Twin Flame looks and feels different than a soul mate relationship. It is the True Love so many of us seek, but it doesn't always happen the way Disney paints it.

Meeting your Twin Flame can be highly electric. The beginning of your Union can be very hot, and include delicious sex, but it doesn't have to fizzle out over time. In fact, it increases and deepens because your Union can support that energy because it's designed to. It doesn't have to go from a hot fire to a warm loving coal over time. It can go from wherever it starts to a sustainably burning flame of love, desire, and passion. It doesn't matter how it starts, it's what it *evolves into* that is important. Why marry someone you had a few years of hot synergy with, only to spend the rest of your life with a person who you feel slightly warm or tepid about? Your Twin Flame Union transcends this pattern and life.

I desired someone who I could spend the rest of my life with, and feel ecstatic about all the way along. I searched for, and created in my life an experience with someone who could continuously evolve with me all the days of my life. I desired and attracted someone who would grow deeper, and deeper in love with me, and with each passing year, we would experience a love greater than we had yet imagined or experienced.

I attracted my Twin Flame because that is what I deeply desired. I desired my Ultimate Lover to spend the rest of my life with. I desired to build and create a life together with her, to create a unified partnership, and live the life of our dreams together. My Twin Flame story may be different from yours, but they can all end the same: with an ever growing, ever expanding, ever deepening Eternal Divinely Unconditional Love. Forget the hot love that fizzles out because that's such a shallow "love." Think a hot love that gets hotter and deeper over time. Imagine a sex life where someone knows and loves you so intimately that they know how to push every hot button in your mind, body, and soul. Think of a sex life that is always evolving, always growing, always changing, and never ever the same. Think of a sex life that is perfectly fulfilling, supportive, and loving for what *you* really want and need. Imagine a life with your Perfect Partner where every aspect of your relationship is designed together by you and your Twin Flame perfectly. Imagine a life where you and your partner love, respect, and support each other all the days of your life.

Know that when you choose to create your Harmonious Twin Flame Union for eternal life, you choose a life of feeling complete in your intimate partnership. You choose a life where your lover is your Ultimate Ally, where you and your partner are always on the same side. You choose a life where you and your Twin Flame are together forever. The dream of Perfect Love is real, and all you need to do to attain it for yourself is to decide you want it, and love yourself enough to achieve it.

What Is Harmonious Twin Flame Union and How to Achieve It Permanently

Harmonious Union is Soul Union. It is the permanent marriage of two into one. This is when, at your core, you and your Twin Flame live one life together. Can Harmonious Union be undone? Not exactly, but if you haven't truly learned the lessons of your Twin Flame journey, you will have to revisit them.

We have had many students come into Harmonious Union with their True Twin Flames, only to leave immediately after, or even months later because they had not fully learned the lessons of their Twin Flame journey. Beneath it all, Twin Flames are an ascension path to God. Yes, they are your Ultimate Lover, but only when you truly understand who your Ultimate Lover is to you, will you finally be able to not only just achieve but *keep* your Harmonious Twin Flame Union permanently.

What is this primary understanding? It is the true awareness that **God is your Ultimate Lover.** Beneath everything, your Creator is your One True Love. Irreplaceable, always there, permanently yours in eternal Union. You are not separate from your Creator, it is God who manifests as your Ultimate Lover, your True Twin Flame. God is not just your Father, your Mother, or an omnipresence floating around far away from your external reality; God is your Divine Lover through your Twin Flame only.

This doesn't mean that just anyone can be your Twin Flame, that you can make love with just anyone because you are with God.

It is easy to mistake another for your Twin Flame if you have not developed the awareness to see yet. It might also be easy for you to think you can make love with just anyone, because you see God in them. This is a great way to leak away your sexual energy into utter exhaustion and aging. Your hair will gray, your skin will wrinkle, and your energy will tire because what is meant for your Union is meant only for you and your Twin Flame.

You see, God is in your Twin Flame, and that is the very Being you love, adore, and desire so deeply. It is God you desire.

Don't worry, we're not here to pull a "bait and switch" on you to turn you on to our spiritual concepts. We're here to simply state the facts as they are. No more, and no less. *God created you and your Twin Flame as two individuals in permanent Union.* You and your Twin Flame are inseparable. And you will ultimately discover your relationship with God results naturally in your relationship with your True Twin Flame.

Shaleia and I have mentioned the term "Harmonious Twin Flame Union" very frequently throughout this book. We first coined this definition back in 2014 when we realized we were experiencing and undergoing a huge and direct transformation in our Union. It was one thing to be together and be living together as a couple, but it's a whole other thing to heal separation from one's Twin Flame at the core; knowing that when you reach this point of consciousness and healing within, there is no going back to experiencing separation with one's Twin Flame ever again. This is Harmonious Twin Flame Union. It is a state of consciousness and

Being attained through healing core separation from your Divine Creator, that is reflected in you healing separation from your Twin Flame. In other words, just like a marriage vow, you promise to be together eternally rather than just in one lifetime or partially in one lifetime.

Many have been, or currently are dating or married to their Twin Flame, but until you invest in doing the spiritual work to heal core separation from the Divine that your beloved Twin Flame is mirroring to you, then at some point, sooner or later you will go back into experiencing separation from your Twin Flame. Achieving Union is not all that difficult, especially after the planetary vibrational shift the Earth experienced in 2012 and the years surrounding it.

Anyone can call in their Twin Flame and meet them, but we have generally always advised against that because it is better and more compassionate for you and your Twin Flame if the spiritual work is already underway in healing separation, rather than call them into your life and try to establish a soul mate relationship with your Twin Flame, or finally do the spiritual work when your Union is in shambles from you trying to go about it the wrong way. Your Twin Flame is the complete opposite of a soul mate relationship because that is not who they are to you, so the old relationship rules will never ever work on you or your Twin Flame.

The secret to attracting your Twin Flame is not just to love yourself, but to take on God as your Lover. When you do this, your Twin Flame reflects that core choice and easily magnetizes into your life.

I challenge you to try this with no attachment or expectations of how your love will manifest on the outside. Just be with God's Love, and the Love you have for God. Miraculous events have transpired from people doing this, including my own life.

The Purpose of Harmonious Twin Flame Union

The purpose of Harmonious Twin Flame Union (HTFU) is to live a God-centered life. This doesn't mean split yourself off from society and pray all the time, it means living in harmony and communion with God with your Twin Flame as One. It means you and your Twin Flame work together to root out the remaining upsets from your One consciousness. It means you live a shared life together of love and romance. All the romance God has for you is expressed through your Twin Flame. That relationship is absolutely sacred, and the sexual Union you share is so private and unspeakably perfect and beautiful, that it could not possibly be shared with another.

The purpose of your Harmonious Twin Flame Union is that you and your Twin Flame live a single life together with a shared purpose. It doesn't mean you have to be working on the same exact thing at the same time, it means you build and grow a life together, an eternal life. Remember, as an eternal being, you keep everything if you decide to reincarnate. Not your physical stuff, but the vibration you hold in your heart that attracts all manner of things to you is kept until you change it.

So rest in solace and peace, knowing you and your Twin Flame get to keep going forever. It is a forever place for your love, an unassailable vessel of protection and security that you may invest in eternally. Its full meaning and purpose is beyond the scope of this book or what can be discussed in any single text. But in a richer medium, like your own Harmonious Twin Flame Union, you can find more there. Ultimately, we choose to impart to you not only your Twin Flame, but a journey of discovery and a permanently open state of mind where richer knowledge and awareness can finally seep in and awaken you always into greater expansion. The purpose of your HTFU is to share a love of Life together forever.

The reason why your initial goal is to enter your Harmonious Twin Flame Union permanently, is not just to finally live One life together physically and spiritually, but because your Union is naturally designed to go to God beyond harmony in Union, into what we call Perfect Union. Otherwise known as ascension.

What Is Perfect Union?

Perfect Union is your complete and total ascension into Christ Consciousness. When you have done the Mirror Exercise to the point where you have no more upsets anywhere in your consciousness, when you have rooted out every last thought of fear in your mind, you have attained Perfect Union.

Perfect Union means you have dissolved all illusions of separation from your Creator and you are One. This would result in a Perfect

Union with your Twin Flame in every way, permanently. There is no going back from Perfect Union once you have sustainably and truly attained it. This is the state of an Ascended Master.

Reaching Perfect Union is simple, but it requires absolute dedication and unequivocal commitment to love. It is your natural state of being as a God-Creator, Child of God, The Most High. You are created in likeness to your Creator, the Source of all things. In Perfect Union, you understand the relationship you share with God: that you are the Child and God is the parent. God is your Source, and through and with God you can do *anything*.

Perfect Union is ascension. It's complete unity and Oneness with the Divine and all of Life, including your Twin Flame. Once you attain HTFU you will soon realize that there should be a natural perfection in your Union free of upsets. All upsets with your Twin Flame (in and out of Harmonious Twin Flame Union) are simply a miscommunication.

You are upset because there is a lack of communication and/or a misunderstanding in communication within yourself. As you clear these miscommunications in your Harmonious Union, you begin to raise your consciousness to Perfect Union where there are no upsets and no communication misunderstandings, because your consciousness is clear, and you have fully united and integrated yourself with the Divine.

What Harmonious Twin Flame Union Looks and Feels Like

Being in Harmonious Union permanently with your true Twin Flame feels like *perfection* in the area of essentially mastering your Divine love life. There is a peace and knowing that nothing is going to come "outside" of you to break you up because there is nothing within you that is choosing separation from your Twin Flame at all. Anger and resentments toward your Twin Flame don't really exist because you know that upsets are an illusion within, and they're coming to the surface to be cleared so you can go deeper into loving and peace in yourself and within your Union.

There's a natural appreciation and gratitude that arises instead of bitterness when your Twin Flame triggers you while you're in Harmonious Twin Flame Union. You notice your foundation growing deeper and deeper, and that sense of security in love you've dreamed of is a self-realized reality.

You look like a couple that is perfect and powerful together because you are, and because you are living your Truth as God has designed you to be. You feel much happier, deeply beautiful, abundant, comfortable, creative, powerful, loved, and self-expressed because you are with ALL of you when you are in Harmonious Union with your true Twin Flame. This way of living feels amazing and very freeing.

Harmonious Twin Flame Union feels like the Home for you that has always existed, and you finally chose to arrive again with your

Divine Lover, when in Truth you never left it. You only believed you did and it's that initial thought that had created the illusion of separation from your Home with your Twin Flame and with the Divine. But upon realizing that all you had to do was heal the core places of separation from your Twin Flame within you, you automatically arrive Home again.

Eight Keys to the Foundation of Your Harmonious Twin Flame Union

Honesty

In order to create anything that is eternal you're going to need the correct foundation. You don't want a foundation about which you are unsure. Why would you build anything on sand unless you intend for it to crumble? In order to know if the foundation is steady it needs to be tested. If there is something there which needs to be cleared, or you find there is no foundation yet, you need to cleanse the debris and form the foundation of your Harmonious Twin Flame Union. Strong foundations are built on trust, honesty, truth, and shared awareness. Strong foundations are built on true love. You build your foundation first by choosing honesty with yourself and your Twin Flame, and then by choosing commitment to your Harmonious Twin Flame Union. You do not need to commit in every single way immediately to one another because building a real friendship comes primary and there are layers of awareness you will receive which you will need to choose to commit to one step at a time. You do, however, need to choose to be completely honest with one another right away. Your Union can crumble easily at the fragile early stages.

Shaleia was blown away when I told her up front that I was committed to total honesty in our Union. I would tell her everything I felt about her and myself, even if it was very uncomfortable to share. I remember one evening after we had moved in together in Hawaii, I told her something very uncomfortable for me to share. I told her I actually didn't like her at all, and I really meant it. I looked into her eyes when I said it and didn't try to cover it up or move away from that statement. "I don't like you," I told her. I then waited for her response without trying to control her or the situation.

She looked back at me hurt and stunned. "Are you kidding me?"

"No," I persisted. "I really don't like you at all. I love you, but the things you choose to do and express aren't really cool with me." I was blown away that I said it. I expected her to be packing her bags and moving back to Sedona soon after I said it. I think she expected the same thing on some level. But there was something very relieving and freeing about expressing myself honestly. It was as if something that was bottled up inside me was able to find release. I was able to let the emotion pass through me and the relationship with her.

By truthfully communicating my feelings and being willing to honor that I felt them, I had expressed my unconditional commitment to honesty in the relationship, and we were able to move through it quickly and reap the benefits of a healthy relationship after that.

No more than an hour later, we were making love, and I had completely moved through the feeling of not liking Shaleia. Honesty is powerful. When we are willing to be completely honest with ourselves and our Twin Flame, then we are choosing love. Dishonesty is weak. It prevents us from clearly and honestly expressing our *true* feelings and emotions and it means we are leaking our power and energy. If you want True Love, you're going to have to choose to honor your *True Authentic Self* and surrender any of your fears to the Divine who guides you perfectly on your spiritual Path.

In the above example where I stated how I honestly felt about Shaleia in that moment, she stood by *her* Truth that she not only liked me, but she was in love with me and wasn't choosing to leave me or herself in our Twin Flame Union. Shaleia wasn't going to accept any other Truth but that which was in her heart in that moment, and she continues to be this way now. Because I know this about her and I know this about myself, there is a deep deep undeniable and impenetrable trust between us, and our Union continues to grow and deepen in Divine Love together.

Your True Self needs to be expressed honestly and your relationship needs honesty to have your *True Self* be part of it. You're not attracting your Ultimate Lover so you can only be half in your Union. You're reading this book because you're an "**all-in**" person when it comes to manifesting your perfect romantic relationship: Harmonious Twin Flame Union. You're here investing your love into yourself, because you're investing in your ability to choose the right partner, and find and keep your Twin Flame in Harmonious Union. If you're anything like me, you've got a lot to share and invest in a person, and you don't want to just dump all that love into a broken glass shattered on the rocks in an empty parking lot. Your love must go somewhere, and grow!

You desire to invest your love into a fortified container that can hold and protect everything you put in it. You desire your love to stay with you. You desire your love to play. You desire your love to stick around and be there eternally. You desire to invest yourself into something and see it come back to you multiplied. You desire to be with your Twin Flame, and be in physical Harmonious Union with them for your whole, eternal life. You desire the Perfect Love that your heart promised you when you were a young child, because it knows your true desire for your Twin Flame, and a child's heart knows Perfect Divine Love. There are some special steps that must be taken in order to attain and maintain that love.

Trust

To get different results we need to take different actions. Harmonious and Perfect Twin Flame Union is built on a foundation of *trust*. A foundation of trust comes from two people coming to the table as their true authentic selves, sharing the deepest parts of themselves honestly, and working together to evolve and grow their Twin Flame Union and HTFU. A foundation of trust *requires* honesty. You can't avoid telling your Twin Flame exactly what you think and feel if you want to deepen intimacy, commitment, and maintain your Twin Flame Union, because you are being honest with how you feel within which develops your self-trust that counteracts feelings of betrayal and uncertainty.

What does honest *not* mean? It does not mean you share every little thing on your mind exactly as you think it. It does not mean you tell your partner exactly how you feel about them when you're extra upset, and really just need to take space and calm down. It does not mean you say things you know are going to hurt your Twin Flame just to purposely hurt them because you are angry, or vent into them, even if you've been thinking this way about them for a while. Instead, just do the Mirror Exercise and resolve it within yourself.

It does mean, however, you have discernment about what you share, but it does not mean you leave out the important stuff. It means you honestly share your authentic feelings, and what your heart is telling you, even if you know it's probably going to be really hard for one or both of you. It means you approach the re-lationship with honesty and *compassion* for one another. It means you respect one another's honesty when it comes out, and you compassionately work through it together. A solid foundation is not built on sugar-coated candy which melts quickly, it's built on bedrock. You're going to need to include absolute honesty in your Twin Flame Union if you want an absolutely unstoppable Union.

Commitment

There's one other key to the foundation of an absolutely unstop-pable Union: *commitment*. Honesty first, commitment is second. Commitment is essential *before* you make it into the Upset stage. **Commitment is what's going to keep your Union strong through the *really* hard times and is a critical component to Harmoni-ous Union.** Without commitment (actually deciding and choosing to be ALL IN with zero backdoor out) you cannot manifest your Harmonious Twin Flame Union. If you're willing to commit to your Twin Flame all the way, if you're willing to commit to seeing the other person through their struggle no matter what, and if you're willing to commit to seeing yourself through your struggle no matter what; coupled with honesty, love and compassion, you have the foundation for an unstoppable Harmonious Union.

With honesty, trust, and commitment as your foundation there is nothing that can stop you from attaining the full experience and expression of your True Love. What could prevent you? You have your Twin Flame, your Ultimate Lover, the one person who will always love you, the soul which has been created for you to love and be loved in return by you, and who evolves with you throughout your eternal journey. There is no higher lover for either of you. Nobody else is going to come along who is better suited for you than your Twin Flame. Remember the truth of this no matter what your circumstances currently are or have been.

If you are honestly communicating everything you are feeling, if you are committed to honesty and trust in your Union, there is nothing that can arise which gets past either of you. No long-term resentments can build up if you're honestly sharing what you both feel. No other person could come into your lives if you are honestly sharing with the other how you are feeling. Honesty creates total clarity in yourself and in your Twin Flame Union. With this total clarity you can see your Union and where exactly it's headed, and decide whether you both like that or not because it's either bringing you closer to your Harmonious Union, or not.

If you desire the foundation of an absolutely unstoppable Union, you're going to need to make a serious commitment within yourself at your core. If you do not commit to yourself getting into your Harmonious Twin Flame Union, then you naturally have already given yourself permission to bow out and give up on yourself, especially when it feels difficult with your Twin Flame, or with the Divine, and you are emotionally triggered. It is safe for you to have faith, trust, and confidence in yourself, your Creator, and your Twin Flame whom you are One with in choosing to commit to this sacred spiritual path of Divine Union.

I'm not talking about getting married to your Twin necessarily, but you're going to need to, very early on in your Twin Flame Union, make some form of genuine commitment you both honor absolutely. Here is an example of the commitment I signed and sent over to Shaleia after a few months of talking with her:

I committed to Shaleia that no matter what happened, I would continue to invest in our Union to the best of my ability and the extent of my power for 30 days after either of us decided to end our relationship. I would give any break-up 30 days before I honored and acted upon it. I would give an extra 30 days beyond what I would give any normal relationship, because I knew there was something special between us that I desired to protect.

I protected my Twin Flame Union with my commitment because I knew I wanted to be sure beyond a shadow of a doubt that ending the relationship was because of a conscious decision, rather than some massive upset that sent each of us hurling down opposite paths at light-speed. My commitment to her, and soon after, her mutual commitment to me, was one thing that kept us together through the most painful and challenging days in our upset stage.

Persistence

In choosing to be with your Twin Flame, coupled with your promise of honesty, trust, and your commitment to your Twin Flame, you will have an unstoppable foundation to your Harmonious Union. In order for your Union to be truly unstoppable you need one other ingredient. This ingredient is the engine behind an unstoppable Union. *Persistence.* Persistence is what keeps you trucking forward even when you're extremely and obscenely upset. Persistence is what pushes the next obstacle off the path. Persistence is the juice that says, "I'm going to keep going forward and investing in my Union anyway." Even when you're faced with the same roadblock again and again and again, and you are having thoughts of giving up on yourself and your Twin Flame.

Persistence is an important key to a truly unstoppable Union. If I didn't have persistence in my Union, it might not have grown very much at all, if ever. We might get stuck in patterns, or quit after our commitment period was over. If I didn't have persistence, my Union might not have the energy to continue through the upsets. You might notice something about the previous statement and lots of other statements in this book, I rarely talk about "we" when I'm talking about my Union. Yes, Twin Flames are intrinsically connected and every choice affects the other, but there's one more special thing about Twin Flames. **You don't need your Twin Flame to**

do any of the healing or clearing work, and you don't need your Twin Flame to read this book for *you* to have an unstoppable Union with them.

When you make a core choice, your Twin Flame is automatically affected and they align to that core choice. You never need to get them to do anything to have a happy and successful Harmonious Union. They will naturally line up with the work you are doing, whether they are conscious of it or not. The reason why this happens is because you and your Twin Flame are One, and when you make a core choice you are making it as One in the place where you are unified. A good example for many people is the core choice and desire to have children. This is why one or both Twin Flames can come with children, or you and your Twin Flame can choose to have a family together when you are united in harmony.

Compassion

Having compassion for yourself and your Twin Flame cannot be stated enough on this journey. If you are lacking empathy and compassion on your spiritual journey to your Union you will find it difficult to attain the vibration of Harmonious Union, because you are constantly judging, angry, and disappointed in yourself and in your Twin Flame. To be unconditionally accepted by your Twin Flame you must have compassion for yourself and what you've gone through to get where you are today and where you are currently headed. Self-acceptance and compassion for yourself and your Twin Flame will fill you up with love and grace because you are loving the part of you and them that is hurting, or didn't know any better, or wasn't ready to choose Union in a place within where you had been choosing and experiencing separation from your Good and your Creator.

Having compassion is essential to cultivating Perfect Union. It is something you must learn along the way and you will be tested on it again and again. Compassion starts with you recognizing no one else can harm or affect you in any way. When you recognize the choices of another, no matter how bad they may be, that they cannot affect you, you can detach yourself from their choices. Even your Twin Flame's choices cannot affect you separate from you, they would only ever reveal your own choices.

Now that you do not have attachment it is safe for you to recognize how painful their upsetting choices must be, or how uncomfortable it must be for them to have to hold on to their upsets. You can have compassion for them. Compassion is not about feeling sorry for another or feeling bad for them, it's about understanding they do not have to feel bad about what they are experiencing, and they can immediately make a new choice when they are ready and release the upsetting experience.

Having compassion for your Twin Flame means loving them so much, you allow them to move through whatever it is they need to go through in order to heal. It means sticking with them through whatever their challenge or experience is, even if you already have the answer and they choose to not listen to you.

One time Shaleia pointed out my business partner was scamming me left, right, and center. I told her I knew what was going on, but I still needed to find a deeper answer. She couldn't understand why I needed to go through with that experience, but she told me lovingly she would stand by me no matter what.

Her loving support accelerated me through my upset and challenge much more quickly than had she not had compassion for me; and certainly much more quickly than if she had tried to place herself in opposition to my desire to complete the lesson. She, and no one else, can truly stand between me and my lessons. I needed to learn it on my own, in my own unique way, and at my own pace. No matter what I had to experience, or go through, I still had to find my own understanding. Her compassion and support made it much easier for me to get what I needed from that experience.

Having compassion for others is very helpful. You're likely to find many people along your journey who are making some pretty awful decisions to experience the illusion of harming themselves. Remember they cannot harm you if you do not choose to invite their choice of separation as your own. You might also recognize what they are mirroring within you, and heal that upset.

You might have to let people go who you once thought were very close to you when you recognize they do not actually align with loving you at your core. The compassionate thing to do in some situations is to let others go so you can truly thrive and come alive. Sometimes letting someone go allows you to find them again in a new, more loving light. Sometimes this even results almost immediately in a much more loving and evolved relationship you both share with one another.

True compassion means you have compassion not just for your Twin Flame and others, but also for yourself. Having compassion for yourself means you do not push yourself beyond where you can sustainably and in a balanced manner go. It means honoring your feelings and honoring where you are. It means loving yourself enough to say "Yes" to choices which are loving, and "No" to choices which are not loving.

This results in a strong, balanced, healthy, and sustainable foundation for yourself, your heart, and your mind, which allows for a rock-solid foundation to grow your Perfect Union upon.

Unconditional Love

Unconditional love is a lot like compassion as described above. It means *no matter what happens, you're going to love your Twin Flame without conditions.* Your Twin Flame is acting like a fool? You love them anyway. Your Twin Flame is saying nasty things to you? You love them anyway. Your Twin Flame is not committing to you and is in a relationship with someone else? You love them anyway. **Unconditional love is the best friend of compassion.**

Once, one of our students had their Twin Flame come to class in Twin Flame Ascension School. She had been our student, and he had been running from their Union recently. We asked her if she would love him without condition if he was kind to her. Of course, her answer was an easy "Yes". Then we asked her if she would love him unconditionally if their romance was going great. Of course, she said "Yes". Then we asked her a much more challenging question. We asked, "What if he runs away again and goes back to his fake wife? Will you love him unconditionally then?"

She felt stumped and stunned. Few people ever think to love someone if that someone is still not committing to them in the moment. Unconditional love means just that, literally. You love them absolutely and unequivocally without condition no matter what.

What happened shortly after that class? They went back into a state of separation, and she became very upset. We reminded her the lesson we had taught her in that very class and she applied it quite diligently. She loved him without condition and had compassion for him as he went through his upset and separation. She held space for him. She didn't withdraw her love from him, even though he had created a strict communication boundary so there was no possibility for contact between them.

Shortly after, he returned with a heart full of love and a lot of upsets cleared. Her unconditional love was a powerful testament to the extraordinary spiritual science we teach in our work. It works every time for every person everywhere. It is normal, it is natural, and it will work fully for you when you put what we teach you into complete and total practice into your life.

Forgiveness

If you desire to cultivate a permanent foundation for your Perfect Union, you'll need to master forgiveness. Forgiveness means "*To let go of completely.*" When you can completely let go of a previous upset with your Twin Flame, you do not free them, you only free yourself. When you choose to hold a grudge upon someone else, you do not harm them, you only harm yourself. Many try or have tried to prove this is a lie, but a lie is a lie and releasing the illusion that holding a grudge doesn't hurt you will always prove that it does, time and time again.

We see so many Twin Flame couples who look like a pair of squabbling ducks who have been holding on to grudges for what appears like centuries. We see them energetically arms angrily folded, looking away from each other and both expecting the other to notice how upset they are, and subsequently change for them. This is such a silly and insane way to go about your Twin Flame Union. If you expect them to change, apologize, or do anything for you to let go of your upset, you are absolutely insane in your expectation. Remember, *your Twin Flame is <u>literally you</u>.*

Maybe your grudges worked to starve the other person of love from your previous romantic relationships, so much so that the pain would shock them into awareness that they would gladly bow to your leverage, but that doesn't work in your Twin Flame Union. Your grudge will only drown YOU in separation consciousness.

When you understand this, you can rise above the pettiness of grudges and transcend to the realm of true forgiveness. This transcendental state is easy to achieve with a simple choice you adhere to all the days of your eternal life. Here is a simple decree for you. State it once through the center of your heart and choose it whenever it arises for you.

"I choose to forgive all upsets past, present, and future any time they arise. Forgiveness comes easily, joyfully, and naturally to me because forgiveness is part of who I am, and extending forgiveness to another naturally extends forgiveness into myself."

This unconditional surrender of a grudge *is* true forgiveness. Unconditional forgiveness is what you really want to master in order to command a complete mastery over a stable, permanent foundation for your Union. Don't worry if this seems like a lot to take in all at once.

If this is your first time reading this book, continue to read through it at a nice pace if you like, and you can always return and study it statement for statement and really meditate deeply upon each idea here. You have an eternity to master this information, and while dragging your feet doesn't serve you, it *does* serve you to take your time and fully integrate everything we are teaching in the body of our work. For it will serve you all the days of your eternal life.

Forgiveness means to let go of something.

In the book A Course in Miracles by the Foundation for Inner Peace, it says that "Forgiveness recognizes what you thought your brother did to you has not occurred. It does not pardon sins and make them real. It sees there was no sin. *And in that view are all your sins forgiven.* What is sin, except a false idea about God's [Child]? Forgiveness merely sees its falsity, and therefore lets it go. What then is free to take its place is now the Will of God" (A Course In Miracles, Workbook Lesson 220, Part II, "1. What is forgiveness", 1).

Learn unconditional forgiveness and you will be transported eternally into the Kingdom of Heaven in this moment, a place where you can fully be present with the Good that is occurring, especially between you and your beloved Twin Flame because you are free from judgment of yourself, and of your Twin Flame.

Respect

Respect means you **honor** *the choices of your Twin Flame, yourself, and others.* It also means you respect the choices of God in your Life through your life circumstances.

If you do not respect what you are experiencing, you are not going to move through it to the next level. If you are experiencing terribly painful separation, you cannot avoid this experience. You cannot taunt or try to bargain with Life in order to get it to change your experience. You must honor what you are experiencing by respecting that you are experiencing it just as it is. It is only from this space that you can move forward through it. This is what brings you your power to change your reality.

Conversely, if you are experiencing a great deal of love, success, and joy, you will need to respect that too. Imagine your Twin Flame is just smitten with you. Imagine you're having an absolutely incredible time together and loving life together. You must honestly respect that this is your experience. If you become woeful and afraid, upset and controlling, hoping to continue this experience, you may choke it of all its wonderful love and Life, thereby actually creating the fear inside you.

Control does not serve you because control has no real power, only the illusion of it. It never has served you. It never will serve you. Your control claims it will provide for you certainty, stability, safety, security, and power. It never ever ever does. It only ever results in loss of what you truly desire. You may experience being in control and feeling good about that, but you will also experience a terrible backlash as a result of this and increased separation from your Divine Good. Control is never, ever, ever worth it. Just surrender and respect your experience authentically and honestly as it truly is.

If you do not respect your Twin Flame's choices, then you are not loving them unconditionally. You are also not having compassion for them. Be sure you respect the Truth in them, and not the lies. If one day, for example, they tell you they do not love you and want nothing to do with you, respect that they are absolutely having that experience. You can do the Mirror Exercise if what they are saying upsets you in any way, and move on while still respecting their experience. They communicated to you that they are experiencing not loving you. Accept this as their experience, *but you do not need to accept this as yours.* See the truth of the situation and transcend the lie and illusion by choosing love instead. Having respected their experience, you are well on your way to helping them transcend it.

With your Twin Flame Union and your understanding of these essential eight principles of the foundation of your Harmonious Union: Honesty, Trust, Commitment, Persistence, Compassion, Unconditional Love, Forgiveness, and Respect, you will truly have an unstoppable Union for the rest of your joyful, happy, and romantic eternal life.

Chapter 7

Your Twin Flame Union:
Life Purpose

Purpose is an underlying motivating reason for which you do everything. Having purpose means you are filled with drive to accomplish, create, do, and express. Having purpose with your Twin Flame in Harmonious Union means you share unified visions, unified goals, and unified needs, which inevitably lead to unified actions. Together you choose your underlying motivating factors, you align your values, and you bring forth all that you both are. You become something more than you were before and you leverage it to create, express, do, and be more than you ever could have, and maybe more than you ever thought possible.

Twin Flames aren't just about having a really hot babe to smooch and love while you're at home. Twin Flames are about having someone you can absolutely align your life with in every aspect because that's your natural design. They're about having your perfect teammate in life, whether it's parenting a family, co-creating a business, or building a particular lifestyle together and/or all of the above. Having a Twin Flame is about having a co-adventurer in life with the one other person who wants all the same things you do, and it means you get to create and share a purpose together. It is so much more than having just a lover; a Twin Flame is your eternal lifetime partner in creation!

Aligning Your Lives

The first thing you'll want to do when you meet your Twin Flame and attain your Harmonious Union is begin to harmonize and align your lives perfectly together. You don't have to align your lives when you first meet, but it's so much juicier, richer, and more intimate if you choose to. If you really desire to create your full Twin Flame experience, you will desire to align every aspect of yourselves because you are aligning ALL of you. You both need to align your life visions and values, and make sure you are harmonizing together as One. You don't need to be married to do this, but you do need to communicate honestly about what you each desire, and how you each feel.

If you do experience conflict, be assured that it's only a miscommunication based on a block one or both of you are having. In spiritual truth, Twin Flames don't actually ever conflict at the core, so that's how you know there's only ever a miscommunication based on a block occurring.

When you and your Twin Flame have communicated each of your desires, values, and life visions, and the choice to harmonize, you will be mostly in alignment. Even if there are some serious disagreements, over time the rifts will fade, and the alignment you share will take precedence everywhere. Shaleia and I spent the first few months of our meeting phase creating shared Google Drive documents, which detailed all the aspects of our perfect home and lives together.

Then we turned our attention to our life's work. Fortunately, Twin Flames manifest as being in perfect alignment in every aspect of life, and career is no exception. This doesn't mean the two of you will always want to do the exact same thing, but it does mean what you each choose will complement the other. Shaleia and I were talking one night on the phone early into our relationship, when she expressed her vision for her life's work. She had always assumed that she and her dream man would be working separately, and returning home to each other at the end of the day. Really, she had never met a man who could match her energetically and spiritually.

She went on to describe to me all the aspects of the career she envisioned, from speaking on stage, to writing books, to doing workshops, etc. I told her candidly that I saw myself doing the exact same things, although I hadn't fully decided upon that path. It took us many more months, nearly a year after we first spoke, before we both sat down and finally committed to our unified career, but it came from honest communication, and mutually aligned values and desires. We're Twin Flames, and we're always going to desire the same things, but we're not always going to be exactly clear on what it is we desire. When one gets clear, so does the other person because choosing to have clarity is a core choice and directly affects your Twin Flame.

Twin Flame Clarity

Getting clear on your desires is one of the most important things you can do in your Union and in your life. When you get clear on your desires, you can make certain decisions and take action toward them. I always desired my Ultimate Lover, but it took a long time, and I had to experience a lot of contrast before I decided upon having my Twin Flame. I would stop at nothing to create my perfect love life. Focusing on what I desired in my love life is what made me successful at attracting my Twin Flame in Harmonious Union. Making a clear decision is necessary in every manifestation, otherwise you weaken the results of what you're manifesting, and being wishy-washy with your intentions will lead you to having wishy-washy results.

Getting clear on your desires for your love life begins the process of attracting what you're specifically asking for, and it can be a journey and adventure all unto itself. You don't need to start out clear, in order to get clear. Shaleia and I had been working diligently on an individual basis before we met, in order to get clear with what we were desiring to experience in our love life. Our culture today sees many young people traveling, exploring, changing jobs, changing careers, changing partners, and changing cities to get clear on what they desire. Many young people have not discovered exactly what it is they desire in their lives yet, so they need to explore and experience contrast in order to gain clarity. This clarity is what brings the success and energy that so many people in society admire. This clarity is what brings any sort of specificity at all.

When you attain clarity, it is easy for you to make a decision to commit your energy and move forward. Until you attain clarity, you can't fully commit to anything for a reasonable period of time. Clarity is what lets us know with absolute certainty that we can move forward and let all the other options go. Clarity is what allowed me to commit to Shaleia with absolute certainty in those first few months. I knew that I desired to spend the rest of my life with my Ultimate Lover, and I knew that she had not yet revealed herself as my Ultimate Lover. I wasn't clear yet on whether I could leave her, even if I wasn't clear yet if I could stay with her my whole life. I was clear enough to make the decision to stay with her until I discovered whether she was my Twin Flame, my Ultimate Lover, or not. I wouldn't have any other woman until I made a decision to follow my feelings all the way to the end. I am still following my feelings, and will continue to do so in my Union every moment of my life.

So how do we get clarity? We explore ourselves and situations, and experience contrast. You don't need clarity on your life purpose in order to be with your Twin Flame. Before I met Shaleia, I was filled with purpose in life, but none of it ended up matching up with what we mutually decided upon as we aligned our Twin Flame purpose together. *What brought us clarity on our Twin Flame purpose together was our mutual exploration of our desires.*

Fortunately for us, we had both done enough personal exploration to get fairly clear on what we wanted as individuals. One thing that really helped us to get clear together was discussion. We got very clear together by discussing our desires, imagining them together, sitting with the imagination for some time, and then evolving the discussion.

We imagined having five children together. After months of discussion and visualization, we both decided we only wanted one child after all. We got clear on our decision to have only one child by exploring all the other options in our imagination that had interested us. Before exploring, I thought I desired a large family, but after contemplating together with my Twin Flame, we both decided a smaller, one-child family would fit better into our desired lifestyles and who we actually are on the inside. Without inner exploration and contemplation, it's very difficult to receive clarity. Without clarity, it's hard to make solid decisions that you can ever commit to.

In order to find your purpose together, you need to create it together based on mutual decisions. When you achieve clarity from exploration, making joint decisions becomes easy. Exploration can be so much fun, and part of the extensive and wonderful adventure the two of you enjoy in life. When it comes time for you both to decide on your purpose together, it will be fun, easy and natural.

Chapter 8

What's the Difference between Soul Mates and Twin Flames?

When learning about Twin Flames and taking the spiritual journey yourself, it can be easy to get confused between a soul mate and your Twin Flame. Both energies can feel so good and similar to each other if one is not aware of the distinct differences. It is important to understand these differences in order to have the awareness to make decisions appropriate for you in your love life. Perhaps you would prefer a soul mate after learning of the challenges of the Upset stage in Twin Flame Union. Perhaps you do not wish to settle for a soul mate after you've learned of the delicious and wonderful experiences only Twin Flames can have together. Whatever you choose, you know the power of your choice is mighty.

God is where I turn first whenever I have a question about anything. I have channeled God's response to the question, "*What's the difference between soul mates and Twin Flames?*" Then I take God's channeled messages, and check them against my own understandings and experiences, in case I missed something, or didn't understand correctly. I also ask God if I understand fully what's being presented to me. This helps me to ensure perfect information to ensure a perfect trajectory of my life's journey.

The Difference between Soul Mates and Twin Flames (Channeled)

Soul mates and Twin Flames are *very different things*, and isn't something you should compare to one another. Today, many people use these terms interchangeably to describe a very delicious and rich relationship, but these are two very different concepts entirely.

Soul mate relationships are not meant to be intimate romantic relationships. A soul mate can be your child, parent, close friend, coach, neighbor, teacher, or special friend. Soul mates are not meant to be in your eternal life forever. They are unique brothers or sisters in God who *resonate closely with you at a particular time in your eternal life journey*. Eventually, nearly all soul mates will come to pass away from you and new soul mates will come take their place.

You will not always make the same choices as the people around you, and so eventually you will no longer resonate in harmony, and you will go your separate ways in your eternal existence.

Sometimes, people confuse a soul mate for someone who you are romantically involved with. Perhaps they were your spouse in a past life, or your spouse for many many past lives. That's okay, but it doesn't mean they were created to *be* your spouse. **They're just a place-holder for your eternal spouse**, your Twin Flame.

We had a student come to us who had one of those so-called "very special" soul mate relationships. She had been married to a soul mate for several lifetimes prior, and it appeared like a very stable, comfortable, easy relationship. Shaleia used a powerful tool she developed called the *Romance Analysis Multi-Reading* to review this soul mate relationship; and the romance was paper-thin, actually, it was a complete illusion. They worked "well" only because they were both afraid of being with their own Twin Flame. When the fear dissolved though through her powerful crystal clear choice to only be with her true Twin Flame, so did their false romance.

Shaleia then reviewed that same client's Twin Flame Union through her *Romance Analysis Multi-Reading,* and the romance was extraordinarily profound. The student quickly let go of the soul mate relationship completely, which was blocking her from meeting her Twin Flame, and her Twin Flame appeared almost immediately. She is *much* more satisfied with her Twin Flame than her special soul mate.

Few people have soul mates like this, but everyone has a Twin Flame. Soul mates are a temporary illusion of romance which ultimately does not last, and few people experience. Soul mates are not the best or recommended romance you can have, because they are not your designed Ultimate Lover, your Perfect Divine Complement, your Twin Flame.

Twin Flames are Divine counterparts to one greater soul blueprint. Twin Flames are whole unto themselves, but completely inter-connected in every way to each other. Twin Flames generally come in pairs, but God can choose to create further, including up to seven Twin Flames in one Union. God does not create more than seven. He tells us it isn't fun beyond seven.

A Twin Flame originates from the Grand Central Sun (God). The Grand Central Sun extends out its Rays (Twin Flame Unions), and these Rays then focus into a flame. So, two or more Flames split from one Ray.

When Twin Flames restore themselves from separation consciousness to form a complete Ray, a *much deeper* love is experienced. The energy which can be expressed through, and between these souls, is tremendous. Everything they experience together in their lives is amplified. Love, pain, emotion, excitement, fear, all expressions, and experiences are amplified in the lives of united Twin Flames.

This is why it can be so difficult at first for Twin Flames to be together. If they have not healed themselves of enough of their separation consciousness to be individually balanced, bringing in their Twin Flame amplifies the upset which they already are experiencing. Some Twin Flames experience tremendous rapid growth and huge upheaval and upset. Other Twin Flames may experience tremendous love and peace. It all depends on where you are within yourself when you meet your Twin Flame.

Just do the Mirror Exercise to clear your separation consciousness and choices, and inevitably, you will experience a tremendous love of your eternal life with your Twin Flame.

Chapter 9

Twin Flames:
Divine Feminine and Divine Masculine
Complements

There are two polarities in Twin Flames and you are either one or the other. You are either 100 percent masculine at your core, or you are 100 percent feminine at your core. These two energies are static in that they remain as this polarity for all of eternity from the moment of your creation.

Twin Flame pairs are always one masculine and one feminine polarity, there is no exception. God created us this way because God is both masculine and feminine, and because the communion of these two energies is *so* juicy.

The masculine energy is a giving, entering energy. It expresses into the feminine from within himself. He desires to express himself lovingly into all he places his attention upon. The masculine is a beautiful complement to the feminine.

The feminine energy is a receiving, abundantly overflowing energy. She desires to receive the masculine and encourages the masculine to give more. The more the masculine gives, the more she overflows into him, thus energizing him. These two energies together are incredibly juicy and extremely powerful. They support and encourage one another tremendously.

When the masculine has blocks to loving, the feminine's encouragement can help him return to a place of giving love. When the feminine has blocks to loving, the masculine can help her clear away these blocks by loving her. The communion is a divine miracle and an utterly beautiful creation of God.

One of the ways you can find out if you are the Divine Feminine or Divine Masculine Twin Flame is by understanding how you best relate to the world. Do you relate through femininity? Or masculinity? You can also arrive at the same answer by understanding how you like to have sex. Do you like to *receive* sex (feminine)? Or do you like to *give* sex (masculine)? It does not matter how your love-making looks on the outside because it is not about sexual technique at all, but rather how you feel and experience sex on the inner levels of your consciousness and being.

Are all Twin Flames male and female pairs? On Earth, of course not! We have many LGBTQ+ people on the planet today who are with their same-sex or other gender-identified Twin Flame. Just because someone identifies as a particular gender does not mean this is the Truth of their Being. Just because someone is born in a male or female body does not mean this is the Truth of their Being either.

Spend a little time researching people, and you will discover there are so many people in male bodies who identify as women, even though they have male genitalia. There are so many people in female bodies who identify as men, even though they have female genitalia.

This is because of a confusion of identification. All LGBTQ+ people experiencing these gender-identification phenomena are experiencing varying degrees of the same inner confusion. Many of these people are experiencing this, and yet are doing fantastic jobs at discovering who they really are inside, and expressing this.

It is important to remember that there are only two polarities, and so ultimately everyone will come to identify with the Truth of their Being. They are either masculine or feminine. Ultimately, there are only two different types of appropriate bodies for each person to experience their Divine Truth in: male and female. This is because the physical body is not just a vessel a soul just happens to "randomly" be placed in, but these highly, intelligently, and purposefully designed physical Earth bodies are created to honor and extend out the true and authentic expression of who you really are inside, as either the Divine Masculine Twin Flame or the Divine Feminine Twin Flame.

But just because you are a feminine energy in a male body does not mean you need to immediately seek surgical reparation for your experience. It is *essential* for you to lovingly accept yourself for where you are right now, and lovingly accept your Twin Flame for where they are right now.

In Divine Truth, you can easily transform your body into the one that aligns most appropriately with your polarity. Our bodies are made up mostly of water. Water can flow and change easily. Be reminded of this any time you are upset at your body. Your body is an extension of your Being. It is not your Being, it is an *extension of your Being.* Somewhere along the way you made choices to transform your body into something different than your initial creation. You mostly did this because you thought it might be fun to explore this idea, and so many others appeared to be having a great time exploring this idea as well.

However, if you are a masculine energy expressing yourself as a masculine energy, this expression is what will ultimately feel *juiciest* to you. It is a thought of separation that you might have more fun expressing yourself in ways that God did not create you to be.

Remember, no matter what you may be experiencing right now, that is absolutely okay. However you identify, that is absolutely okay and there is no pressure to change in any way. If there is anything our global consciousness has hopefully learned at this time through the LGBTQ+ movement, is unconditional acceptance and respect of self and others no matter what they are choosing.

We do not expect you to change in any way, but we do find it important to clearly communicate the very simple Truth of your Being. This is not a book on discovering what polarity you are on a deeper level, but search your heart and your experiences if you are unsure. You can explore and experiment, try new things, discover who you really are inside.

Ultimately, it does not matter what anyone else thinks, says, does, or chooses, you must be satisfied and happy with yourself. You must feel good about yourself and your choices, and no one else can have any say in that whatsoever. At the end of the day, it is you and you alone who you must be with for all of eternity; and the thoughts, choices, and words of others should have no bearing whatsoever on how you handle your relationship to and with yourself.

Seek to always honor your True Self within though, and you will always find utter peace, joy, satisfaction, and self-acceptance for all eternity. In honoring yourself, you will find it easiest to be with your Twin Flame. In fully accepting yourself and loving yourself for where you are right now, you will find unequivocal joy, peace, and acceptance from your Twin Flame and your Union. Choose to honor yourself completely, and there you will always find love.

Chapter 10

Colby and Keely's Twin Flame Love Story

First Meeting
February 2017

Colby

We wanted to open up, but we felt afraid. There was so much that could go wrong and so much that had gone wrong in the past. How could we suddenly fall in love and have a perfect life? How could all of our problems be solved in a moment? It made no sense. And yet, there we were, looking each other in the eyes, with a knowing that this is what we had been looking for our entire lives.

We were both unsure of where this amazing person had come from. We met, awkwardly, behind the meat counter at our local grocery store.

The next day, I noticed that I had an undeniable urge to be around her. I wanted to talk to her and get to know her. So, every chance I got, I was in her work area, doing her work for her so she had the space to share her life with me.

We talked about everything. Politics, spirituality, climate change, music, our past, our current relationships, our childhoods. The conversation flowed as we caught the wave of our passion for each other.

It wasn't long before our conversations began spilling over into the night. Keely offered to give me a ride home at the end of our shift and I immediately accepted. This quickly became a trend.

Keely

The walls around my heart melted instantly when he was around. He was very quickly and suddenly becoming my closest confidant. I was struck by how natural and easy our relationship felt. I could talk to Colby about anything and everything under the sun. No topic was off-limits. Not even my passionate rant about gender and sexual equality could scare this man off. I was humbled.

I could feel him stare right into my soul when we talked. He saw everything about me and that scared me a little. I tried to keep him at a distance, but Colby saw past my fear. He was persistent.

I always knew when Colby was working. He wasn't afraid of being heard. His loud, booming voice could be heard echoing off the concrete walls.

I couldn't get him out of my head even if I tried. Something inside of me knew that my life would be forever changed by our relationship.

Colby somehow sensed when I was done with work even when I wasn't working in his department. He would search for me through the grocery aisles because he knew that I liked to do a little shopping after my shift.

When he found me, I tried to play it cool like I hadn't already been thinking about him. He stared fearlessly into my eyes with complete focus. I had no choice but to surrender to his love. He was into me and it was mutual.

Time stopped when we were together. The sounds and images around us blurred away as we spoke about our days, our favorite foods and drinks. Usually, a customer would ask him for assistance and our conversation ended. I'd make my way to checkout with Colby's presence still on my mind.

Colby

Every time I entered the meat department, I would check to see if Keely was there. She did the same. We were totally aware of what was occurring within each of us. We were just hesitant to admit it.

As the month progressed, we both realized that our current relationships were doomed. I had a fiancé and a one-year-old at home. I released layers of shame and guilt as I followed my heart to Keely. Nothing could convince me to let her go. Our relationship felt too good to pass up.

Claiming Eternal Love
April 2017

Colby

Keely was the first person I felt completely accepted by. We shared the same interests, dreams and outlook on life. She had everything I had ever wanted in a woman and more. She encouraged me to follow my dreams and spoke in ways that felt familiar.

Over the weeks, my fiancé sensed a shift in me. I was happy for the first time in a long while. I was finally saying "no" to misery and "yes" to love. Once she realized she could no longer control me, she left. Breaking up was the most compassionate thing to do. We were not created as eternal lovers and we both knew it. No matter how hard we tried, our relationship was not meant to last.

Keely

I was having deep upsets with the boyfriend I was living with. I started looking online for answers on how to save our failing relationship. That's when I came across "Twin Flames." I remembered seeing Twin Flame videos the year before. I thought, "Maybe we were Twin Flames?" According to the videos, all I had to do was wait and, eventually, he would come around.

I gave him space while I focused more of my attention on myself and my own happiness. I didn't want to wait to feel good. As I continued loving myself, we barely saw each other. We were more like roommates than boyfriend-girlfriend. I kept watching Twin

Flame videos on YouTube and one psychic assured me that by the end of the month, my man would return.

The end of the month rolled around and our relationship only felt worse. I realized that I had been holding onto expectations of what I thought our relationship was. I chose to let my expectations go and love him unconditionally. I went all in and I claimed him. Our relationship felt even worse after that.

My relationship with my "friend" Colby felt so much better.

The more I loved and accepted myself unconditionally, the less my boyfriend wanted to be around me. Then it dawned on me. I loved myself more than my boyfriend loved me. I broke up with him that night and I chose to claim my true Twin Flame. I knew he was out there. I didn't care who it was, what body they were in, or how old they were. All I wanted was to be in a healthy, loving relationship. I was done with separation.

Colby

I was eating my burrito outside work on my lunch break when I saw Keely walking my way. She had her work boots on with black jeans and her small black REI backpack. Her hair was tucked away under her beanie. She looked cute.

As her eyes caught mine, her face lit up in a smile. She stopped at my table to talk.

"How are you?" Keely asked.

"Um, it's been interesting. I'm letting go of a lot of fear these days," I replied.

Keely looked at me inquisitively. "Mhmm," she replied.

"How are you?" I asked.

"I'm doing great! My boyfriend and I just broke up and I feel free. I realized how much I had been holding myself back from living my life," Keely responded.

"Wow. My fiancé and I just broke up too," I replied with a big smile on my face.

"Oh wow," Keely said with a perplexed look on her face.

Despite our attempts to maintain our relationships with other people, they disintegrated. At the same time. And now we were both available. It was time to make my move.

Our First Date
May 2017

Keely

I was working in the receiving dock when Colby showed up outside my office. I was listening to spiritual videos when he arrived.

I blushed and pulled out my earbuds so I could hear him.

We got to talking as we usually did, and the conversation turned to our future. My lease was up at the end of the month and my plan was to quit my job and live off of the money I had saved up until I figured something else out.

"You're never alone," Colby blurted out.

His words hit me right in the heart. Tears began forming in my eyes. He meant that with his whole being.

"Thank you," I replied. "That means a lot."

"It's true. If you ever need anything, I'm here," Colby said. Time seemed to stop.

"Hey," Colby said with a glint in his eye. "Would you want to come over to my place and hang out?"

Before I could even think, I said, "Yeah! I'd like that."

Colby

When she arrived, I was putting my daughter down for bed. Keely patiently waited in the living room for me to finish.

I was very happy to see her. I knew this was a big deal and I was finally with the woman I really wanted. I invited her into the backyard.

Quickly, I gathered wood and started a fire. The flames began to climb as we gazed into the fire. The dusk sky gently illuminated our faces as the sun sank below the horizon.

The energy flowing through us was electrifying. We continued to converse as we had become accustomed to. There was no mistaking the connection that we were both feeling. Something deep within us both had awakened and was rearing its head. There was nothing we could do but continue to get closer.

Keely

As the night progressed, I could no longer deny my feelings for Colby. He was the one I had been looking for, and he had been right here all along. I read him his astrology chart and talked with him about spirituality. He looked at me with love in his eyes. That's when he leaned in and asked if he could kiss me.

I said, "Yes!" despite my nerves. As our lips met, I felt a deep surge of energy rise within me. Our first kiss was electrifying, yet peaceful. It just felt *right*. Fear began to clear from my system as I realized who Colby was to me. He was my Twin Flame.

Colby looked at me with a grin on his face and asked if I'd like to go on a walk. I quickly agreed. We held hands as we walked the peaceful neighborhoods around his house. I gazed up at the stars twinkling above us. As we walked, Colby stopped at each tree and spoke to it. He would tell the tree how beautiful it was and how thankful he was for its presence in our lives.

At first, I was a little embarrassed. I had never been with someone who was so unafraid of being himself. I let my fear of being seen go. I, too, shared a deep love for nature and I thought his relationship with trees was endearing. He loved the trees and was not afraid to show it.

The following week was pure bliss. We had stepped out of the lives we knew and into another world. As we spent more time together, a sublime connection with the whole Universe began to show itself.

Day in and day out, we were together. We were floating on a cloud, our troubles left far behind. We knew that this is where we wanted to be. We knew that we belonged together.

By the end of the week, we were discussing how we were going to move in together. We had plans to start a healing retreat center; we would design the landscape using permaculture principles and have meditations and discussions to help with emotional trauma.

It felt like everything was falling into place, but there was something essential missing. We didn't have the healing foundation we needed to manifest our dreams.

Separation
June 2017

Keely

Then we reentered the world we had known before. We began interacting with the people whom we had had relationships with. Colby's friends and family were wary of our connection. Fear began to show itself. Doubt began to creep into our minds. And we allowed it to fester. Was this just another "too good to be true" tragic love story like all the rest?

Colby

It doesn't really matter what it was that broke us apart. The specifics never really matter. All that matters is the choice between love and fear. In this moment, we chose fear.

Despite all of the glory of our friendship and the depth of the feelings we had for each other, we broke up. Keely got in her car and drove away. And I chose not to fight for her. We allowed our dreams to slip away.

We spoke for a brief period after Keely left Portland for her hometown in Massachusetts. This did not end well, as we believed we had a fundamental schism in beliefs. We did not talk for several months after.

Keely

Choosing to leave my man was the absolute worst decision I've ever made. I wasn't aware of what this relationship really meant and I attempted to treat it like any other relationship. I have deep compassion for myself here. I thought I could get over Colby by distracting myself with a three-month-long road trip down the West Coast. What I learned is that I absolutely could not get him out of my heart and soul. I also learned that I could not stay mad at him.

Lessons Learned
August 2017

<u>Keely</u>

The further I drove, the worse I felt mentally, physically and emotionally. Eventually, my health conditions were so bad that I could barely do basic tasks. Living alone in my car was no longer an option. My parents offered to have me stay with them. I was relieved to have a stable place to stay where I could recover and get the medical help that I needed.

Shortly upon arriving at my parents' house, Colby and I spoke again. After our phone call, I was hit with a wave of sadness as I realized how seemingly far away we were from one another. I felt empty inside. I knew we needed to be together, but I wasn't quite sure how.

I was pointed to the elephant in the room: my physical health. I had depleted myself so severely over the last few months that my body felt really out of sync. I could no longer digest my food without pain, bloating and constipation for days. I started seeing a nutritionist and found out after taking an allergy test that I was allergic to almost all the foods I was eating. I was afraid of food and feeling hopeless. I knew I needed to get my health in order if I were to go back to Portland and be with Colby.

The next several months consisted of me trying all sorts of "remedies" for the pain like eliminating sugar, meat, dairy, and all processed foods. I began smoking medical cannabis several times a day to ease the pain, but soon realized that this was not the answer. I didn't want to be reliant on cannabis. What would happen if all the cannabis ran out? What would I do then? I thought to myself, "There must be another way. There has to be a better way to live my life."

Finding Our Teachers
April 2018

<u>Keely</u>

I stopped smoking and started feeling again. Things I had tried to suppress came up. One of those things was my deep and undeniable desire to be with my Twin Flame. I was finally coming out of the fog and into the realization that I had enough of the contrast. At that moment, I chose happiness. That's when I found Jeff and Shaleia on YouTube. Seeing them for the first time on YouTube was a moment I will never forget. My whole consciousness buzzed in recognition of who they were to me. I felt like I had known them forever.

"They are my teachers," I said in my heart.

I started binge-watching all of their free content. I watched as Jeff and Shaleia were living the life I had just barely tasted several months ago. I was determined to learn everything they had to teach me.

Whenever I was feeling particularly depressed or hopeless, I would pick a YouTube video from Jeff and Shaleia's channel, curl up under a blanket, and allow their words to soothe my soul. Their videos were so different from the other Twin Flame "teachers" out there. Jeff and Shaleia knew something that these so-called teachers did not.

In one particular video, I remember listening to Jeff and Shaleia talk about how one of the keys to coming together with your Twin Flame is recognizing your oneness with God. This statement struck a chord deep within my soul. I had a flashback to my time with Colby and how at peace I felt. At the time, I was just recognizing a higher power of perfection that ran through everything within and around me. I called this power the Universe, Gaia and Mother Earth. I realized after hearing Jeff and Shaleia talk about God, that I had really been talking to Him the whole time!

I didn't grow up religious. My mother was somewhat spiritual and believed in an afterlife and my father was an atheist. "God" wasn't a term I was familiar with. Growing up, I envied my friends who practiced religion and congregated at their church on special occasions. The sense of community was always something I desired.

Another one of Jeff and Shaleia's videos advertised their Twin Flame school and Facebook group. I immediately joined their Facebook group and found out that I could become a member of Twin Flame Ascension School and Life Purpose Class for just a couple hundred dollars a month. I had just enough money to pay for both monthly memberships. I knew in my heart that this was the solution I had been looking for.

There was not a single ounce of doubt in my mind. My whole being knew. I began studying Jeff and Shaleia's classes and the Mirror Exercise on a daily basis. My weekly discussion group was something I looked forward to every week. I finally felt understood.

The difference this community made on my journey was everything. I was able to talk to actual people about what I was experiencing without judgment. Not only that, but they provided me with real, grounded solutions to all of my problems. Things in my life started changing rapidly as I learned how to love myself for the very first time.

Reconnection
June 2018

Keely

My health greatly improved as I felt my feelings and reconnected with my body after years of abuse. I attended a body healing session and we healed the core of my digestion issues. I allowed myself to eat what I wanted for the first time in my life and I had no adverse effects. My digestion is now better than it has ever been in my entire life.

Three months passed and I was feeling better and better each day. I felt real Peace for the first time and I began developing a loving relationship with God. It was God that brought me to Colby and it was God that brought me the solution to my desires: Jeff and Shaleia.

Everything felt lighter. Even my family relationships improved. I mirrored my previous upsets with Colby and chose the truth each time. I forgave myself for leaving Colby and chose to have compassion for us instead. Everything was going so well. That's when God told me it was time to reach out to Colby.

I almost resisted, out of fear. But then I decided to choose love. I chose to trust God and with God's guidance, I sent Colby a seven-minute-long voice recording over email updating him on my life and deeper awareness. I made the choice to allow God to speak through me.

I told Colby that I love him and that I haven't stopped thinking about him. He responded four hours later with an email. One of my favorite things he said in his response was, "I can hear your peaceful solitude in your voice. It is unmistakable and refreshing. Good job." I was very happy that he noticed my spiritual progress. We both agreed that talking on the phone would be a good next step.

Colby

When it came time for Keely and me to talk on the phone she did not pick up. I called several times, but her phone just went straight to voicemail. "She stood me up," I thought to myself. I was used to being treated this way by other people, but I was surprised to experience this with Keely. It didn't seem like her to do something like this. I chose to work through my feelings and thought that there must be a good explanation.

Keely

I was nervous about my "phone date" with Colby. I chose to romance myself beforehand to help calm my nerves and feel connected to God. I chose to dress up in a beautiful flower-printed dress and do my hair and makeup. I sat on my chair, looking out the window as our agreed upon time quickly approached.

Several minutes passed and I had not received a phone call from Colby. I felt a slight panic arise within me. "Oh no... he must not be interested in me," I thought to myself. But then I began mirroring my upsets. I chose to love the part of me that felt abandoned and hurt. God never left me. He is always here. An hour went by and still no phone call from Colby.

Eventually, I slunk downstairs to the living room. My sister, Marlee, was waiting for an update. I told her what happened and she calmly asked, "are you sure he's not blocked on your phone?"

"Of course not," I replied. "I unblocked him months ago."

Marlee looked at me, still questioning me with her eyes. "Maybe you should just double-check," she said.

"Okay, I'll check, but there's no way..." I trailed off in disbelief when I saw that Colby was indeed still blocked on my phone. I hit the unblock button and then my phone was flooded with old voicemails and text messages from Colby over the past few months. This whole time I thought he wanted nothing to do with me was really just my own fear of being loved.

Back in the beginning of 2018, I felt so desperate for contact with Colby that I ended up blocking him on my phone so that I wouldn't be tempted to send him needy and annoying messages. I could've sworn that I had unblocked him back in April, but apparently not!

I immediately texted Colby my apologies and told him that I was available to talk with him now. He replied right away and answered my call.

Colby

When Keely and I spoke on the phone for the first time in several months, I felt very peaceful and grounded. Despite feeling frustrated earlier about our mishap, I chose to forgive her and love her regardless. I could tell that we were both doing exactly what we were meant to do. Even though I did not have the words to describe it, I knew that she was my Twin Flame. I had an indelible feeling in my heart.

Keely

While on the phone with Colby, I decided to do a visual meditation with him. I guided him to his heart space where I helped him picture the heaviness on his heart start to unravel and release in love. As I guided him to his heart, I could feel all this energy rise up from my chest, into my throat and then eventually release through my crown. I started crying and told Colby that I loved him. He said it back.

Later on, Colby told me how overwhelmed he felt by all these spiritual changes. He described how he felt like he's been in a cocoon for the last few months and has been experiencing ego death after ego death. I made the choice to have compassion for our healing process and asked him if he'd like me to walk him through his upset.

When I asked him to find the part of him that was feeling overwhelmed, he said he couldn't see it. I told him not to worry because I could and would heal it. I described the part of him that needed love and encouraged Colby to love himself there.

The next morning, Colby told me how spot on I was about the upset. He asked me to bear with him as he figured this stuff out.

"I'm not going anywhere," I responded.

Colby

We spoke for three hours while I sat under a Western Red Cedar. I remember her describing a candle in her bedroom. The flame was split in two for a moment and then merged into one. I knew that this was our destiny. I felt a lot of admiration as Keely talked about her spiritual practice and the community she had become a part of. Keely mentioned that she was going to take a trip to my city soon and I was very pleased at the thought of seeing her again. I told her that coming back to Portland was a great idea.

The Reunion
September 21, 2018

<u>Keely</u>

I received my Romance Report from Jeff and Shaleia. It blew my mind. When I read the channeled message from my Twin Flame, I immediately started crying and felt my heart opening up. It was safe to open up to Love again. One thing that really stuck out to me was when Jeff told me that I didn't need to master my total Ascension process in order to be with my man. All that is required for me to succeed is to work through whatever is arising now. In order to do that, I must accept myself where I am right now. This brilliant piece of information was exactly what I needed to prepare for my potential reunion with Colby.

The plan was to travel across the U.S. to Portland, OR with my sister, Marlee and to help her move into her new dorm. Colby knew I was coming, but we hadn't solidified any plans to hang out. I had lots of fear and anxiety coming up, but I remembered Jeff and Shaleia's advice. All I had to do was to accept myself. That was enough.

Colby

When the time of Keely's arrival neared, I was scared and felt unworthy of such deep love. I sent Keely an email and told her that I shouldn't see her because I thought I was not worthy. She quickly called me and left a message saying that my sentiments were nonsense and she was really looking forward to seeing me. I felt her love through her words and felt a lot of ease enter my body. I knew she was right.

Keely

Colby's message scared me at first, but I knew that I had all the tools I needed to heal our consciousness. I called out his fear and loved him. Nothing was going to stop us from being together.

The next day, Marlee and I packed our bags into our dad's minivan and drove to the airport. I had six hours of plane time before I could see Colby. I chose to use this time to feel my feelings and love myself. At times, the anxiety was so strong that I felt like giving up, but I refused to make the same mistake I had made the year before.

I came back to my place of peace and read passages from the *Autobiography of a Yogi* and, of course, this book. I knew God was guiding me the whole time and I had nothing to fear. I chose to surrender to Him.

Later in the flight, I felt called to treat myself to a cheese and fruit platter and a beer. I had never bought alcohol or food on a flight and worked through feelings of unworthiness. I asked God to help me through the resistance and he pointed to my neighbor's book titled, "The subtle art of not giving a fuck." I laughed and felt the energy within me shift. God has a great sense of humor. It was the perfect message I needed to honor my desire to love myself without fear and judgment.

My food came immediately, but my drink was nowhere to be seen. I wasn't upset about it because I was perfectly content with focusing on my food first. After about 30 minutes, the flight attendant that I placed my order with came around. I reminded her of my drink order and she immediately apologized. I could tell she felt bad about it so I assured her that it was okay and not to worry.

"Bless your heart," she said and she came back a few minutes later and told me she would not bill me for any of my purchases to compensate for the inconvenience. I felt so loved and taken care of. I love how God loves us. All we have to do is claim our support.

Colby

My daughter, Avalyn, and I set out to meet Keely at the airport when her plane landed. I was terrified as we navigated the airport. "Am I good enough?" I kept asking myself. Shortly after, I found myself gazing into her beautiful blue eyes once again. Her open acceptance put my paranoia to rest.

Keely

Marlee and I were getting our luggage when I heard someone yell, "Excuse me, Miss!" I turned around to see the most beautiful man in the world. He was with his two-year-old daughter, Avalyn. I greeted them and then embraced Colby for a long and well-earned hug. I felt at "home." I then pulled out a beaded bracelet with a dragonfly that I had made for Avalyn. It fit her perfectly.

Colby was so sweet. He helped us with all of our luggage and offered to drive us to our destination. As we were walking through the airport, I felt so grateful to be in the presence of my Twin Flame. We started toward the escalators and Colby went in front of us with two of our largest suitcases. He looked back at Avalyn and I could tell he was wondering how he would be able to take Avalyn with him.

This was my cue to step up and claim my role as his partner. Just as I made the choice, Avalyn grabbed my hand and we walked over to the escalator as I helped her on. I was nervous. I knew Colby was watching me. Avalyn and I successfully boarded the escalator while Colby watched in relief.

I was still a bit nervous around Avalyn. I felt unsure of how to act around her. I didn't have much experience being around two-year-olds, so I chose to surrender to God's lead. I chose to claim her with all my heart. I chose to be there for her and mother her exactly how God intended me to. I felt honored to have the opportunity to love Avalyn and be a part of this family.

When we got to Colby's car, he lifted all of our luggage into the back. It felt so good to be cared for like this. I released resistance as I chose to receive God's support through Colby.

As we drove to the city, I saw so many license plates with our initials that I couldn't help but giggle. He looked over at me with an inquisitive look. We chatted a little bit, but mostly we just enjoyed each other's presence. It was a surreal feeling. I felt like no time had passed since we were last together a year ago, yet so much had changed. I had the power of God in my heart and the teachings of Jeff and Shaleia as my guide.

We arrived at our destination in downtown Portland. Cars and people buzzed around us. All the new students were gathering around the Portland State University campus and I wondered how we'd be able to find a parking spot. Just then, a car put it's blinker on and pulled out in front of us, leaving a parking spot behind. Colby and Avalyn helped us unpack all of our luggage and walked us to Marlee's dorm room. It was time for Avalyn's nap, so we said goodbye and parted ways.

Later that night I felt called to get takeout and bring it back to my Airbnb, which was only eleven minutes away from Colby's house. God told me it was time to make a move. I was guided to send Colby my address and invite him over for food and drinks. I got over my initial reluctance, surrendered, and sent him the message. I reminded myself of Jeff and Shaleia's teachings and how my good is here. All I need to do is claim it and have faith in God. Colby immediately replied.

Colby

Shortly after Avalyn and I arrived home, Keely invited me to join her at her Airbnb. "That sounds lovely. I'll be over at 8:30 pm," I replied with feelings of excitement moving through my belly.

Keely

After I felt clean, comfy and nurtured, I ventured out to a liquor store three minutes from my location. I originally went in for a beer, but God guided me directly to the wine section and straight to a bottle of Cabernet Sauvignon with three ravens on it. Ravens and crows reminded me of my first year living in Portland. Next, it was time to get some Thai food. The woman behind the counter asked if I wanted extra rice (no charge). I happily accepted. I gave her a big tip and left with a smile only to realize when I arrived back at my place that she had also given me a delicious side of mango rice pudding. Everything was unfolding so perfectly.

Five minutes after arriving back at my place, I received a call from Colby telling me he was close by. I waited for him outside.

Colby

I arrived at Keely's Airbnb. When I saw her, I couldn't help but stop and stare. She was the most beautiful woman I had ever seen. She was wearing dark red lipstick and a choker necklace with a beautiful orange stone on it. Her Airbnb was cool. It was its own mini sanctuary located in the backyard of a larger house.

"It's called *The Garden Home*," Keely said with a smile. "I booked it with you in mind," she added.

Her voice made my heart flutter. Her smile was enticing. Every time I looked her way I could feel my heart opening up to her. Keely invited me to sit with her next to a mini wood stove.

"You look really good," I said as I gazed into her eyes.

She blushed and thanked me.

Keely pulled out some takeout containers and told me she had ordered Tom Ka soup and offered me some. I laughed and told her that I had just ordered that earlier for lunch. We both smiled at the synchronicity.

Keely

After a little while of chatting and sharing food, I decided to give him the gifts that I had brought with me. The first gifts I presented to him were two jars of homemade tomato sauce made with tomatoes and vegetables I grew on the farm I worked at over the summer. One jar was smoky, spicy and sweet and the other one was made with heirloom tomatoes and had a lighter, refreshing flavor. Colby thanked me and told me these gifts were "fit for a King."

I pulled out my next gift, an oracle card deck about love. Colby had never seen an oracle deck before, so I gave him a little overview and pulled a card for us. It was the card "Heaven." I read the guide and poem that went with it. Afterward, we were both just smiling into each other's eyes, feeling the Love all around us and within. He told me that the card was exactly what he needed to hear and that it was one of the most beautiful passages he's ever heard. He gazed at the deck in amazement as my heart fluttered with joy. I knew he'd love it. I then gave him a copy of *Autobiography of a Yogi*. I had mentioned it about two months prior and told him it was well worth the read. He smiled and thanked me graciously, but then admitted that he had already bought a copy after I had first suggested it. I was flattered and pleased to hear that he took my recommendation to heart. I told him that he could just give that copy to someone he felt guided to.

"I'd rather give someone the one I just bought so I can keep the one you gave me," he said. I blushed again. A few moments after, I suggested we maybe go on a walk and he said "of course." I then told him that I was desiring a glass of wine and asked if he wanted any. He declined. As I was pouring a glass for myself, he told me that he had actually said "no" out of fear. I giggled and asked him again. This time he accepted.

We eventually found our way onto the floor in front of the heater. At first, he sat diagonally across from me and then realized he was uncomfortable and scooched over next to me. We began talking about God, our spiritual work, and all of the progress we've made. We sank further onto the floor as we both found peace. We started meditating together in silence as we surrendered deeper. At one point, I slipped into sleep and woke only to find Colby still meditating. I smiled and felt so comforted and loved at that moment. This was exactly what I had always dreamt of.

After adjusting ourselves again, we realized that we no longer desired to go on our walk. We were perfectly content with staying in and enjoying the warmth and comfort of the indoors. We found our way back onto a bench chair at the edge of the bed and we both just sat there staring into each other's eyes. The tension was building and we finally leaned in for a kiss… which turned into a wonderful makeout session.

The rest of the night was so healing. Our fear and self-judgment began melting away as we surrendered to our love for one another. Colby looked at me directly in the eyes and said "I'm yours, my love."

"I've always been yours and I have never left," I replied.

Back to Massachusetts
September 23, 2018

<u>Colby</u>

The time came when Keely needed to get on a plane to head back to Massachusetts. Neither of us wanted to let the other go. This time, however, we weren't going to let the other get away.

<u>Keely</u>

I waited outside underneath an overhang and watched the rain fall. Colby pulled up in his truck and I felt the reality of the situation sink in. He asked me how I was doing and I immediately started to cry. He lovingly held space for me and reminded me of the truth.

"Our love is limitless and it never leaves," Colby reassured me.

I thanked him and worked through my feelings. Once we got to the airport, that's when Colby began sobbing. I comforted him and held space as we hugged each other. I knew that everything was going to work out. I remembered our teachers' words, "Love never fails." I repeated them out loud. We hugged, kissed and cried together.

That's when God told me it was time. It was finally time to give Colby the book I had been desiring to give him all along. My favorite book of ALL time: *Twin Flames: Finding Your Ultimate Lover* by Jeff and Shaleia.

I told him how Jeff and Shaleia are the reason for us coming together. Without them, I wouldn't have found a way to truly heal. I also reassured him that the book would help explain our relationship. He smiled while graciously accepting my gift.

Colby placed his hand on my heart center and said, "my love is right here anytime you need it. You can always find me here." I thanked him and I told him how much I loved him and that I would be coming back very soon.

"This bond is unbreakable. We are one," I said as I left his truck. Later during my flight, I received a text from Colby sharing a passage from Jeff and Shaleia's book, "Happiness and joy is not something you find by having something in the future, it is a choice and realization that can only happen right now within yourself." I later realized that I was on the exact same page.

Union
September 27, 2018

<u>Keely</u>

The next few days were rough. I attempted to do work and un-pack, but I couldn't. My focus was on how I was going to get back to Portland. In that moment, I realized how much I had been holding myself back from Life. God was in total support of my Twin Flame Union and had always been. The only thing holding me back was my choice. I chose to stop the suffering. I chose to commit my whole heart to God, myself and my Twin Flame.

A few minutes later, I received a message from Colby asking if we could talk on the phone. I told him all about my breakdown and breakthrough and how I was done keeping myself from Love. He greatly appreciated my honesty and shared similar sentiments. I told him that I committed fully to God, to him and our union and he repeated the same back to me. Then God prompted me to ask him something I had always wanted to ask.

"So God asked me to ask you if I could call you my boyfriend?" I awkwardly asked.

He chuckled, "Of course. As long as I can call you my woman," he said confidently.

And so it was. Peace fell over us as we both felt relief with this deeper level of commitment. It was exactly what we both had been desiring all along.

After posting my update in the Twin Flames Universe Facebook Open Forum, Jeff confronted me about my choice of separation from my Twin Flame. "Why not go and be with your man?" he asked.

A bunch of excuses came up in my mind. I had already committed to the entire growing season at the farm I worked on. I was also just about to graduate my nine-month herbalism course and only needed one more class. I then thought about my family and how they would miss my presence and the extra support I provided. After listing out my excuses I realized that this was my test. I had just chosen to go all-in with my Union. Was I going to put my Union first or put my life on hold to appease other people? I chose Union.

The next day I informed my work, family and teacher of my decision. The decision may have seemed "sudden" for them, but I knew in my heart this was the only real choice. Being with Colby was my main priority and I wasn't going to let anything get in the way of that this time. The next few weeks consisted of me creating a budget, selling my car, packing up my room, searching for jobs in Portland and talking to my beloved.

Colby

We spoke on the phone every day, sometimes for hours at a time. 2,000 miles wasn't going to keep us apart. During our numerous conversations, Keely shared the teachings of Jeff and Shaleia with me. I asked for the login information to her Twin Flame Ascension School classes and immediately dug in.

The first time seeing Jeff and Shaleia in the recorded classes was like seeing someone I had known, but hadn't seen in a very long time. I recognized them. Their words permeated every cell in my body. I knew they were my teachers.

Keely invited me to become a member of the Twin Flames Universe: Open Forum on Facebook and I was welcomed with open arms. I had never been a part of such a supportive community before.

In order for Keely to come back to Portland, she needed to fly across the country without having a job or a place to live. It wasn't possible for her to move in with me, so she planned on staying at Airbnbs until we figured out something else. This required great faith. Keely and I chose to believe.

I had many doubts about whether this move would work or not. I was afraid that Keely would not get a job and would spend all of her savings and then have no money and no place to live. But Keely constantly reassured me that everything was going to be okay.

"God's got our back," she said.

I felt the truth of her sentiment and agreed to her plan. I picked Keely up at the Portland airport shortly after. All of our fears melted away as we embraced once again.

Back for Good
November 2018

Colby

We had been through so much over the last two years. Now we were together and we knew we would stay together. There was nothing that either of us wanted more.

As the days passed, the reality of our situation began to set in. Keely had to get a job fast and we needed to find a place to live. We did not panic. We had faith in the strength of our relationship and in the power of our Creator.

Everything that we needed to be supported started to fall into place. Keely got the exact job she wanted and we began searching for a home. We had several factors working against us in our search for a viable home. Nevertheless, we persisted, submitting applications and touring several homes. None of them seemed to fit, so we continued our search.

No matter what, we never lost hope. We never threw in the towel and said "this is too hard." Giving up was not an option. So we persisted.

It was not long before we found a viable option. We contacted the landlord and took a tour. It was not perfect by any means, but the landlord was quick to approve our applications and send over the lease agreement. We signed, paid, and received the keys. Just like that, we were moving in.

We felt like we had just completed a magic trick. There was this feeling of having overcome the most difficult circumstances either of us had ever faced. Finally, we felt like we could relax. Our relationship had withstood the test of time and hardship. We celebrated our first night in our new home in high spirits, a young couple settling down to a life of love and accomplishment. Nothing could stop us.

Living Life Together as One
December 2018

<u>Keely</u>

Colby and I slept on a twin-sized blow-up mattress for the first night living together. Our budget was tight at the beginning because I had to wait three weeks to get paid at my new job. As we settled in, we managed to find a Queen mattress set on Craigslist for cheap. It was quite the upgrade.

One day I came home from my usual morning shift to find a table and chairs in the kitchen and our bed made up for me. Colby knew that I usually took a nap when I came home from work so that I could rest before needing to pick him up after his night shift. I felt so loved and supported by God. Living with my Twin Flame is so easy and fluid.

As we continued to do our inner work and move forward, a miracle was bestowed on us by our gurus, Jeff and Shaleia. They called the Twin Flames Universe community to come together to support our Union financially. At Jeff and Shaleia's behest, a fundraiser was begun, and over $5,000 was gifted to us. We could not believe the immense generosity of our community and the immense love we were receiving. But there we were, receiving all of it. We graciously received the money and put it to use paying off our debt and creating a home. The support we received through this sum of money was not just material, but spiritual as well. Our lives were once again transformed by Jeff and Shaleia. This is only one instance among many.

Our process was swift and decisive this time around. Whenever there was a decision to be made, we made it. We never toyed around with ego, entertaining its lies. There was only one path to follow: Love. If that path was shrouded with wilderness, we unsheathed our machetes and hacked our way through. There is no force in the Universe that can stop us, least of all our own minds. We let go of our aspirations to be anyone other than who we are right now, for who we are in this moment is perfect.

The belief, both in our own abilities and in our relationship with God, has led us to great things. But there is no way we would be here if it weren't for our gurus, Jeff and Shaleia. Through the darkness, they shined a light. Through the waves, they showed us the land. Through the misery, they showed us love. No matter where we go or what we do, our success will always be their success.

One of our greatest successes was the achievement of our Harmonious Twin Flame Union. We were given the miracle of Harmonious Union in our first live class with Jeff and Shaleia in December

2018. A feeling of bliss and harmony began to wash over us both as we sat listening to all of our fellow students describe what defines Harmonious Union. Our persistence through our struggle had brought us so many miracles, each greater than the last. Now, we were about to receive the greatest of them all. The realization that we were in Harmonious Union brought us such great peace and joy, as we understood what all of our efforts had been for. We had finally arrived home.

At every turn and through every upset, we continued to go deeper and choose love. No matter the cost, no matter what we had to release, we put all of our focus on God and love. And we received the reward for our dedication.

Attaining Harmonious Twin Flame Union was my dream the moment I entered Jeff and Shaleia's school. I knew it was for me, just like they said over and over again. It was my relationship with God that got me through every challenge. He led me directly to Jeff and Shaleia, and they led me directly into the arms of my beloved.

The Engagement
January 27, 2019

<u>Keely</u>

A month later, we were engaged to be married! Colby proposed to me under a giant Douglas fir tree in the woods near the coast of Oregon. It was absolutely perfect. Our life together only grew stronger as we continued to deepen our relationship with God.

Colby planned the most perfect day for us. We started our day at Tillamook State Forest and hiked around for a few hours. It was magical. Toward the end of our hike, we came to a fork in the road. There, a large spruce tree with beautiful green moss hanging from it took my breath away. My mouth dropped as I felt the Divine presence of God flowing through the large branches of the tree and inviting me in. Colby started taking something out of his pocket and I asked if he was going to take a picture. He smiled and said "no" and pulled out a jewelry box instead. I immediately started crying. I knew exactly what was happening (in fact I had known for a while... it's hard to keep secrets from your Twin Flame lol). He got down on one knee and asked me to marry him. Of course, I said "yes" and I cried some more as he placed a beautiful blue sapphire ring on my ring finger. We embraced and held each other for a few more moments while we wept. It was everything that I had ever wanted and more. A real dream come true.

The Big Day
September 2019

Colby

Just as we were engaged under a tree, we were married under a tree. A slight drizzle fell upon Keely and me, as we held hands and prepared ourselves to commit to one another as husband and wife.

Keely

Exactly one year after coming into Twin Flame Union, Colby and I chose to marry. The previous year felt like the shortest year of my life. It was filled with some of the most challenging and miraculous moments I've ever experienced. Our ascension journey had greatly accelerated since living together. We treated each day as a day to go deeper with love. And that is exactly what God called us to do on September 29, 2019.

We desired for the wedding to be really simple and peaceful. It was perfect for where we were in our lives. A big wedding party with lots of guests and expenses just wasn't compassionate at that time.

God kept telling me that Colby and I would get married in September. I didn't really see how that would be possible, but God's plan is always so easy and clear when we choose to surrender to it. The small wedding party was everything that we desired for our special day. Our officiant was so loving and kind. She helped us find the perfect spot to get married outdoors, near the water and under the trees. She was patient and understanding with our busy schedules and encouraged us to do what we felt was best in our hearts.

Colby and I decided not to write our vows beforehand. We both desired to speak freely from our hearts. A great sense of completion entered our beings as we gazed into each other's eyes.

"Awwwww," cooed Avalyn, as we professed our undeniable love for one another. Everyone giggled.

Mother Nature looked on as we sealed the deal on the life of our dreams. As we were sharing our vows, I heard a "quack" and looked down to see a family of ducks arriving to witness our special moment. Avalyn was also very amused by the ducks.

After the ceremony was over and all was said and done, Colby and I went back to our house to rest and ground. We celebrated with a lovely sushi dinner at home and relaxed on the couch for the remainder of the night. Besides the upheaval, we felt really peaceful and grounded in our choice to make our marriage official. It felt extremely relieving to align with what we knew in our hearts.

Colby asked me if I could've imagined marrying him a year ago. My answer was "no," but because of my spiritual teachers, Jeff, Shaleia and Grace, all my doubts and fear around marrying my True Twin Flame were completely dissolved. There's no room for doubt in the Kingdom of Heaven. Anything you desire is already yours. You just need to follow the teachings of Jeff and Shaleia and claim it.

Our Hearts Are Fulfilled

Keely

We feel deep purpose in sharing our Harmonious Twin Flame Union and marriage with the world. Being an Ascension Coach has always been a dream of mine. I rejoice in the success of others and I receive so much healing from each session. All of our clients are perfect. They teach us so much about God and always give us the next piece to work on. Without sharing this work, I would be lost. Without your Life Purpose, there's no point in being with your Twin Flame. Sharing Jeff and Shaleia's teachings brings both of us deep and satisfying peace. It fills us up.

Helping others into Harmonious Twin Flame Union has brought our Union purpose and is really the only reason we are still together. Our coaching business has brought us much abundance in the form of wealth, too. We are blessed to be able to work from home, create our own schedule, and share in the healing of this work every single day. There is not a day that goes by where we are not working and healing for both our clients and ourselves. It is a part of who we are.

Aspen
November 2019

<u>Keely</u>

Shortly after we married, a group of our dedicated clients gave us an all-expenses-paid trip to Aspen, Colorado. We were in awe at the generosity of our friends and clients. Colby, Avalyn and I had just come back from a family apple picking trip and made a choice to claim our family deeper when we received the gift. The gifted trip was intended to be for Colby and I to ground in our marriage with the very generous option of bringing Avalyn. We chose to claim Avalyn on a deeper level and share this massive gift with her.

Colby

The trip was magnificent. Aspen was absolutely breathtaking and our room was elegant and very supportive. Both myself and Avalyn went skiing for the first time, and Keely gave me some good tips. We were put up in a beautiful 2-bedroom presidential suite next to a pool and hot tub in a 4-star ski resort. We had literally EVERYTHING we needed. We flew first class (first time for me & Avalyn), received ample support from the resort, ate healthy food and did loads of spiritual work while our clients and friends supported us. I felt undeserving at times but I knew that my test was to receive God's love here. God really loves us. All of us. A LOT. It's safe and normal to receive so much love and to leave poverty and abuse behind. In fact, it's insane to resist it.

This trip opened our eyes to the truth of our wealth. We are not meant to be poor. We are meant to be wealthy, and it is a simple task to open to that reality. Staying in Aspen showed us the ease of this task.

As we committed to ourselves on a deeper level, we also became more aware of our relationship with my daughter, Avalyn. Regardless of whether Keely is Avalyn's biological mother, we are both her parents. Avalyn sees Keely as her mother and Keely sees Avalyn as her daughter. I feel absolutely blessed to have a wife who is so committed to giving Avalyn the childhood that she both needs and deserves.

We apply Jeff and Shaleia's teachings to every aspect of our lives. The same core principle: "Love Yourself" is deeply applicable to parenting. When we love ourselves and give ourselves what we need, this love overflows into Avalyn's life naturally and abundantly. We are only able to be attentive to Avalyn's needs when we are attentive to our own. We are learning how to be parents, but not just any parents, we are learning how to be Divine parents.

Being Divine parents requires an awareness of our own Divinity. How can we expect to guide anyone to their Divine nature if we are not in touch with our own? Our lessons in parenting have been lessons in getting to know ourselves. We have released our expectations of how we believe parents are supposed to look and have chosen to trust God's direction instead. We learned to invest in ourselves first, and only give to Avalyn from a place of genuine relationship. This, in turn, has empowered Avalyn to make her own decisions and embrace her own divinity.

Our Lives are Constantly Expanding

Keely

Our most recent addition to the family is a beautiful German Shepherd puppy, named Teyla. She loves playing in the grass, eating lavender flowers, chasing soccer balls, chewing on her toys and snuggling with her family. We knew instantly that Teyla was the one. She wouldn't leave my side. When I gave her to Colby, she melted in his arms and licked his face.

Colby and I love being dog parents. We've been working really great as a team, preparing our house and grounding in our new routine. I love going outside more and waking up earlier. Teyla absolutely adores Avalyn and Avalyn is very happy to have a play-mate. It feels really good to have a dog that can be active with the family and teach us all deeper discipline.

As we grow and expand, we can help others do the same. The more we support ourselves, the more we can support all of our relationships. Jeff and Shaleia teach that we live in the Kingdom of Heaven. Harmonious Twin Flame Union is a deep recognition of this truth in all areas of our lives.

There is so much joy in our lives now. We have truly arrived in a place of outpouring abundance. Every day as we work, we feel the presence of God guiding us through each task. We are living the life of our dreams, and it was easy to accomplish by following Jeff and Shaleia's teachings.

Throughout our journey, we had several moments of doubt and insecurity. Moments where we believed we had been abandoned by God. When these doubts arose, we thought it was the end of the world. We even let these doubts confine us to opposite ends of the United States. It seemed like our lives had ended.

But, through the work of Jeff and Shaleia, we found our way back into our hearts. There we found the strength and truth that we required to see through the veil of suffering. God told us that we are meant to be together. We listened. Then we acted.

We chose to claim our Harmonious Twin Flame Union. We chose to let go of ego and only pursue happiness. We stopped at nothing to accomplish our dreams.

Through every block, through every challenge, we continued to listen. Obstacles were overtaken and conquered one by one. There is nothing that could have stopped us from being together. Our tenacity and commitment won the battle against our upsets.

We healed every ounce of separation that was keeping us apart and chose to transcend it using the Mirror Exercise and having a solid relationship with God. We left behind the old, dingy house with a crooked landlord for a spacious, clean and supportive home. We felt like our car was too small for our growing family, so we bought a Mercedes SUV. Our Union was facing blocks to romance, so we healed them. Our business needed more clients, so we manifested them. There is not one area of our consciousness that we have not invested in and improved drastically.

But it is not just us making the effort. At the heart of all of this improvement is God. The gifts that we have been given is a modest indication of the infinitely rich and abundant relationship we have chosen to have with God. Our foundation is not the Mercedes or the nice house. It is our relationship with God. This is what enables us to be successful at everything we do.

No matter what hardship we were facing, we never turned our backs on God. And now, we enjoy the fruits of our relationship with him. But this simple relationship with God is our source of joy and happiness. And we enjoy it in infinite abundance.

As we continue on our journey, we rest easy knowing that all is well, and all will be taken care of. Such is the nature of a healthy relationship with your Creator.

With this work, I am constantly in wonder of how my life is un-folding so perfectly. All of my wildest dreams are coming true. From getting married to my one true love to fulfilling my dream of being a spiritual healer, moving into a nice new house, providing Avalyn with a childhood I could've only dreamt of, getting a new puppy and purchasing our very own Mercedes Benz. Our lives have completely changed for the better. We are blessed to share these gifts with all and we bless you, the reader and your Harmo-nious Twin Flame Union, too.

Twin Flame Decrees

NOTE: These are not casual decrees. These decrees are channeled directly from The Divine Source. They are imbued with Divine Love and Divine Healing Energy. Repeat each of them once from the very center of your heart and you will experience their full effect. You need not repeat them again once you have decided, however you may find pleasure and enjoyment in regularly repeating them at your desire.

"I choose to be in Permanent Harmonious Union with my True Twin Flame."

"I surrender my life to God's Loving Way. I choose to see, know, and completely accept God's Loving Way when it is presented to me. I choose to follow God's Loving Way with absolute faith, commitment, dedication, discipline, and joy. I trust God to show me The Way."

"I surrender all of myself completely to Love's Warm Embrace. I trust love will guide and protect me, and I protect and channel only love in my every thought, word, choice, and action. I am One with Love in every moment now and eternally."

"I am God's Perfect Channel. Whenever God calls me to, I will speak, act, and choose as my Creator asks. I act immediately upon God's Loving Guidance without hesitation or laziness. I am complete in my love with God."

"I choose to manifest my Twin Flame now for the purpose of Perfect Union and my Ascension. I choose to align myself fully to my Perfect Union and take all steps needed to permanently secure my Perfect Union sustainably for all eternity. I am One with my Twin Flame and together we choose to enjoy an eternity of loving enjoyment with God as One."

"I take each step in my Ascension journey with peace, joy, ease, and loving perfection. I surrender all resistance and patiently work through each step as it arises. I am One with God's Love now."

Twin Flame Poems

How Love Sees

In the flowering bud of my Heart
Love emits its sweet fragrance into the world
As I open only to Love
I receive only Love
And I give only Love

Intoxicating forth the presence of immaculate perfection and beauty
I am enraptured and embodied by the sweet nectar of my true love

I see now, how love sees
I hear now, how love speaks
I feel now, how love feels
I understand now, as love understands

That in which I sought in another
I have found within myself
I have found within God

Written by Shaleia
a few days before her initial reunion with Jeff in 2014

Love Was Always There

I knew it first in my heart the moment I recognized the desire,
The feeling of Love.

I felt it first in my center and I knew.
All I knew was I knew.
The feeling of Love.

Then somewhere along the way I forgot,
I brushed it off, let it slip away.
The Truth of Love.

And my life hurt. Life hurt me, it hurt to live.
But I kept living.
I kept living to find my Love.

***

I had forgotten what it was like to Love,
but Love whispered to me
Love's Eternal Call.

Love was always inviting me forward where
Perfect Love awaited.

I searched far and wide, under every rock and shade of tree,
and still it felt far away,
Yet Love's call remained in me.

Love always seemed so close yet it never moved,
always waiting and present in its abiding whisper.
Love was always there.

***

When I finally began to venture within,
I found things I didn't like, but I held strong with faith.
Love guided me through.

I touched things I had thrown away,
and I finally put them in their place.
Love strengthened me along the way.

And when I arrived back home to Love,
I knew it was me who had left,
but one thing never changed:
The Truth that Love *always* remains.

Now I know to never leave, never to stray again,
because with Love I go everywhere and I know
Love is found within.

Written by Jeff
in May 2017

Afterword

Remember, only love is real and love *never* fails.

There is a problem you will run into now, having finished the book. Maybe you won't run into it because you're already an incredibly refined spiritual master who only needs a slight turn into love and then everything becomes right for you. But perhaps you need a little more support beyond this. The Truth is, all the work has been laid out before you in this book. Nothing has been left out. Nothing is missing. Everything is here. You need nothing more. The heart of the work is now yours. The real problem is your programming.

You see, even though this book holds infinite power, it is still only a tiny bastion of unshakable information which stands lovingly and relentlessly against the illusions you hold. Your mind is great and vast and likely filled with much which would stand in the way from the love revealed in this book, which would maintain your illusion of separation from your Twin Flame for eons to come.

We have already foreseen this and have worked diligently to provide you with a larger body of work, an incredible and rich experience which will overwhelm the illusions you may still hold, and return you elegantly into Perfect Union with your Twin Flame. We are not here to only provide you with a tiny opening to Heaven, but instead, a vortex of irresistible love that dissolves all illusion. The resources you will find beyond this page will transform your life in even more powerfully supportive ways than can be contained within the pages of a book.

The more you lovingly support yourself on your Twin Flame Ascension journey, the more easily things will come to you. We invite you now into a deeper relationship with us, that we may lovingly guide you further on your spiritual path. Take our hands, choose to lay down your fears, and allow us to guide you all the way Home. We invite you to continue with us at TwinFlamesUniverse.com, and allow your Twin Flame journey to blossom to its fruition so its nectar may bless the world as it blesses you in return. Amen.

Sincerely and in Divine Love Always,
Jeff & Shaleia

Recommended Materials

By Jeff and Shaleia:

- *TwinFlamesUniverse.com*
- Online Facebook Group Community – Twin Flames Universe: Open Forum
- Twin Flame Ascension School recorded online classes at *TwinFlamesUniverse.com/TwinFlameAscensionSchool*
- Twin Flames: Dreams Coming True e-Course
- Twin Flames: Romance Attraction e-Course
- Twin Flame Healing Meditations (MP3) by Jeff and Shaleia
- Life Purpose Class recorded online at *TwinFlamesUniverse.com/LifePurposeClass*

Others:

- *A Course in Miracles* by the Foundation For Inner Peace
- *Autobiography of a Yogi* by Paramahansa Yogananda
- *The Divine Romance* by Paramahansa Yogananda
- *How You Can Talk With God* and *The Law of Success* by Paramahansa Yogananda
- *The Essential Rumi* translated by Coleman Barks
- *You Can Heal Your Life* by Louise Hay
- *Bhagavad Gita*
- *The Radiance Sutras* by Lorin Roche
- *The Secret of Love: Meditations for Attracting and Being in Love* by Deepak Chopra (album)
- *The Laws of the Spirit World* by Khorshed Bhavnagri

About Jeff

Jeff is a passionate explorer of God-consciousness and a Twin Flame spiritual teacher. He stumbled across the subject of Twin Flames after he uncovered his in pursuit of his own Ultimate Lover. He consciously and deliberately seeks to understand and uncover the secrets of life through deep inner awareness of himself and his environment. He is willing to ask questions,

 discover new pathways, and pursue his desires in unique and creative ways which lead to specific and measurable results. He married his beloved Twin Flame, Shaleia, in January 2016.

About Shaleia

Shaleia is an eternal spiritual teacher who is aligned to the teachings of Christ Consciousness. In her writings, YouTube videos, classes, and courses, she conveys a simple yet timeless and powerful message: Heaven is not within you, Heaven IS you, and there is a way to live the Truth of your Eternal Self now in Harmonious Union with your beloved Twin Flame.

Shaleia meditates daily, and brings her peace, wisdom, and knowledge out into the world for the benefit of All. She enjoys hiking in nature with her camera in hand, along with her Twin Flame, and goldendoodle by her side.

Printed in Great Britain
by Amazon

38656856R00128